A GIFT FOR

D0116554

_____

FROM

_____

Blue Epiphany

The Book of Comforts

Simple, Powerful Ways to Comfort Your Spirit, Body and Soul

Ideas
Personal Revelations
Inspirations
Quotes
&
Art

By Patricia Alexander & Michael Burgos, MFT

Artwork and Design by Dean Andrews

The Book of Comforts™

Copyright © 2005 by Michael Burgos and Patricia Alexander, Blue Epiphany

P.O. Box 192, Templeton, California 93465, (805) 479-7778

Original Art Copyright © 2005 by Dean Andrews, Marina Del Rey, California 90292

Aerial photography on poll pages by Don Farrall/Getty Images.

Portrait photography by Wayne Smith, Ventura, California.

The information in this book is true and complete to the best of our knowledge.

All recommendations are made without guarantee on the part of the authors or Blue Epiphany.

The authors and publisher disclaim any liability in connection with the use of this information.

For additional information, please contact office@bookofcomforts.com or go to

www.bookofcomforts.com.

ISBN: 0-9773229-0-4

Printed in China

DEDICATIONS

I dedicate this book to my lifelong friend, Hannah the Curlyhead, who taught me that consciously choosing to comfort yourself can be an act of courage and survival.

PATRICIA ALEXANDER

I dedicate this book to my mom, whose willingness to listen unconditionally made her a blessing and a comfort to all who knew her. (Plus, she always said I could write a book.)

To my father, who provided many comforts for me, including his loving protection.

And to Johnji, who comforted me when I thought I couldn't be comforted, and without whose care I wouldn't be here today.

MICHAEL BURGOS

For my mother, the artist and inventor, who leaned over me with approval in her heart, encouragement in her voice, and wonder in her eyes.

DEAN ANDREWS

ACKNOWLEDGMENTS

We feel deeply grateful to our family and friends (among others, Bill and Susan; Cas, Susie, Christina, Jeffrey and Julianne; Russ; Margaret; Shelene and Tayler; Helen and Bob) and all the people who responded enthusiastically to both the concept and the creation of this book. You made us feel like this was not only a good idea, but an important one.

Author Michael Broggie graciously gave us his time, expertise, and a few secrets about the art of publishing and selling books.

Patricia's son, Mike Norquist, did an excellent editing job, with insight, good English, and the perspective of an intelligent young man in his twenties, all valuable contributions.

Sona Vogel of New York, Patricia's dear friend and a professional book editor, gave the manuscript its final tightening while giving us her unbridled enthusiasm.

Author Cheryl Canfield, who started as an e-mail and phone acquaintance, became a real friend. We thank her for being so generous with her expertise, her time and her tender heart.

Inspirational author and seminar leader Angeles Arrien met Michael and instantly saw him as someone with something important to say. She graciously offered to read this book and comment on it for our back cover, which she did with her special spirit of inclusiveness and love.

Under threat of dire repercussions, we must thank Randolph Scott Burgos, the best (if grumpiest) comfort teddy bear in the world; and Ender and Valentine, the best comfort cats and teachers of comfort, bar none.

And lastly, our heartfelt thanks to all of you who answered our survey question, "How do you comfort yourself?" We were impressed by the careful thinking that you put into this topic and the fact that you took the time to write out your answers and e-mail them to us. Your thoughtful responses will be a comfort to many.

WHY WE NEED
A BOOK ABOUT COMFORTS

People are desperately seeking ways to comfort themselves.

We always have. The need for comfort crosses all spans of time and all boundaries: race and religion, gender and geography. We have always sought ways to relieve the pain amassed in our spirits, bodies and souls.

Today's rapid world, however, presents new pressures. Our phones ring in our pockets, multimedia pronouncements of doom are in our faces, and anti-anxiety meds are in our pillboxes.

Our technology tempts us to adopt distraction as comfort, investing our lives with behaviors that are numbing and addictive. Our "human condition" – a physical body with intricate thoughts and feelings – makes us forget that we are spiritual beings.

Distracted, we underestimate how real relief from stress is vital to our inner balance, and just how accessible relief can be. Ironically, it is often when we need authentic comfort the most that we are the least equipped to find it.

Our hope is that this book will give you something you need – simple and powerful ideas from real people for ways to comfort yourself that are healthy and meaningful.

And, most of all, ways to comfort yourself that will make a difference at those times when you are least able to think of them yourself and, thus, need them the most.

CONTENTS

To need comfort is to keenly feel an imbalance in one or more of
the three arenas that define our humanity: Spirit, Body and Soul.
Here are powerful, yet simple ideas for thinking, feeling and being
in better balance, divided into these three vital areas
that determine who we are and how we live.

SPIRIT

*The part of a human being characterized by
self-consciousness, intelligence and personality.*

BODY
The entire physical part of a person.

SOUL
*The vital essence or heart of a person; the animating,
individual force of a human being, often believed to survive death.*

SPIRIT

THE PART OF A HUMAN BEING CHARACTERIZED BY SELF-CONSCIOUSNESS, INTELLIGENCE AND PERSONALITY

You cannot have a proud and chivalrous spirit if your conduct is mean and paltry;
for whatever a man's actions are, such must be his spirit.

DEMOSTHENES
Athenian Orator and Statesman
384 – 322 BC

It is not likely that posterity will fall in love with us,
but not impossible that it may respect or sympathize;
so a man would rather leave behind him the portrait of his spirit
than a portrait of his face.

ROBERT LOUIS STEVENSON
Scottish Novelist, Essayist and Poet
1850 – 1894

1

2

CREATE ANTICIPATION
1

There is no medicine like hope,

no incentive so great,

no tonic so powerful

as the expectation of something tomorrow.

ORISON SWETT MARDEN
American Author
Founder of *Success* Magazine
1850 – 1924

It's A Comfort To Create Positive Anticipation

Give yourself what you need.

If the days are spinning by too quickly and looking too much alike, that's a sign you need to create more things to enjoy in your future. The fact is that we always need something special that we can look forward to in our lives.

We've all heard of people near death who maintain the will to live until something happens that they're waiting for – a visit or a birthday – and then die shortly thereafter. That's how powerful the act of positive expectation is to our spirit.

What's amazing about anticipation and its impact upon us is that it can be about large, less common events, like a vacation; midsized, semiregular occurrences, like going out to dinner with friends; or small personal pleasures, like watching your favorite TV program or looking at new photos.

It's important to realize that you yourself may need to make plans to create the events you will look forward to experiencing. For instance, utilize your own birthday to set up a get-together with your friends and loved ones rather than expecting them to create this for you. Be proactive in setting up a day, a week, a year that you'll look forward to living.

So calendar in something that will get your heart beating. And after that's done, calendar in another.

IDEA Take out your calendar once a week to schedule some fun. Having something to look forward to takes both planning and awareness of things that give you pleasure, like a romantic evening with your partner or a round of golf with your friends.

4

These things rarely happen by accident. You have to whip out your calendar and look at the next month and then the next three months, and then look at the rest of the year. Start thinking: What is it that I want to do this year that I can look forward to? Don't just let life roll along – it will roll right over you and be on its way – leaving you behind and wondering where the time went.

IDEA Create a present box. You don't have to wait for someone to give you a present. Every now and then, buy a little something for yourself that you like, gift-wrap it and put it into a Present Box. Whenever you feel kind of blue, open one of the gifts. The odds are you won't remember what's inside them and it will cheer you up to rip off the paper and get a prezzie just because you need one!

IDEA Set up a daily reward system. We're all like the proverbial donkey: We go forward a little faster if there's a carrot dangling in front of us. Life is full of chores, deadlines and responsibilities. It's also full of distractions, pleasures and joys. To not overdo either category and stay in healthy balance, set up a daily carrot for yourself. You get to watch your favorite show after you've taken out the trash. You're off to your favorite shop after you've cleaned that room that's been messy too long. You get to go out to dinner with friends after you've made a work deadline.

Present Yourself With A Gift You've Earned

5

Look At Your Calendar For The Year

Create some travel plans that excite you.

Michael:

I love to travel so much that Patricia calls me her Marco Polo. Each of us has something like this that energizes and motivates us through the mundane quicksand of life. Nothing gets me more revitalized than a trip to my local bookstore to peruse the travel section and create an outing that I can look forward to every couple of months.

It only takes five minutes of viewing beautiful places and interesting adventures for my heart to start racing with excitement. I live to pick out several different-sized trips I can plan for the year ahead. I can climb out of the doldrums by looking at travel catalogues with big color photographs or surfing the Internet for great trip ideas. I see railroad journeys into Canada or car trips to the local mountains and think: I'm ready! I want to go!

One of my favorite ways of setting up my travel carrot is by looking at significant times on my annual calendar. These include birthdays, graduations and business deadlines. I use these reasons to celebrate as opportunities to create memorable experiences.

For instance, for my 47th birthday, I'm thinking about going to the North Pole. No, really, I am. You can do these things in the 21st century – it's an amazing time to live. And traveling lets me know that I'm not only alive – I'm really living.

I live to pick out several different-sized trips I can plan for the year ahead.

…traveling lets me know that I'm not only alive – I'm really living.

Plan A Trip

6

Meet Your Own Needs When You Can

Enjoy small gifts that cheer you up.

Patricia:

I learned something very important from a wonderful young woman who let me sleep on her couch one night.

My former husband and I had decided to separate shortly after we moved to a new city, but were unsure of how to run the logistics. Ann, a church acquaintance, offered me the hospitality of her tiny apartment while he and I figured things out.

Ann told me her story: She had survived a troubled youth, with an alcoholic mother and an absent father, only to marry an abusive, alcoholic man. Finally divorced, she struggled with alcoholism and low self-esteem. To top it off, she had a serious heart condition. Despite all these gut-wrenching obstacles, she appeared upbeat and cheerful. Everyone at church adored Ann's gentle ways and supportive presence.

"You need something to cheer you up," she exclaimed, and brought out a long plastic box from under her bed, filled with wrapped gifts. She urged me to choose and open one. The gaily wrapped present revealed a necklace – not expensive, but pretty. The gift was so unexpected and sweet, it did cheer me up.

Ann explained that as she learned how to live a more emotionally healthy life, she realized she could give herself what she needed. Whenever she felt sad or had something to celebrate, she pulled out the present box, filled with little things she'd bought and wrapped, and gave herself a gift.

That night I learned that depending on myself could be the best gift of all.

As Ann learned how to live a more emotionally healthy life, she realized she could give herself a present whenever she needed one.

That night I learned that depending on myself could be the best gift of all.

Look To Yourself For The Gift Of Caring

7

How Do You Comfort Yourself?

Margaret, 75, Inspirational Speaker and Entertainer/Performer
   I actively try to spot a story or an ad about places that would give me pleasure to visit, such as 50 acre gardens or a museum event. I tear out the story and plop it into a pretty little white bowl that has a most appropriate saying written on it: I Love You. When the time comes that I need to baby myself, these little slips of paper are waiting to remind me of just what I might do to deliver myself from dis-comfort.

Greg, 52, Computer Consultant
   I like to take a walk.

Jane, 61, Artist
   I like to go wandering through stores, sometimes in strange cities, usually on a hunt for something I don't need. Sometimes a friend will give me an object to search for. I feel immensely satisfied when I find it, but the search is the soothing thing. It is better than a glass of wine; it's a total escape that can last hours or weeks or even years.
   Sometimes I just get a magazine with fabulous pictures and go out for breakfast while I look at it and dream awhile.

Note Everyday Successes

Victories abound in everyday life.

Michael Burgos

It's A Comfort To Note Your Everyday Successes

Find the validation you need.

There's no better confirmation that we have value as human beings than when another person acknowledges us. Yet, if that's our only source of self-esteem, we will live entirely at the mercy of others and their ability to be good communicators and gracious givers.

Frankly, we're all pretty self-involved and not all that focused on validating others. It's not unusual for our successes and talents to be taken for granted.

On the other hand, it's also easy for us to take for granted some acknowledgment that is there, but that we devalue or ignore.

Victories abound in everyday life. So give a comforting boost to your self-confidence by taking notice of your own victories, whether others do or not. And start catching those acknowledgments that you may be deflecting without even realizing it.

IDEA Think about why people love you. Take a moment to look at yourself through the eyes of those who love you. Why do they feel affection for you? Choose to feel good about how your love translates into tangible actions.

IDEA Read your own résumé. Sometimes there's nothing like taking out that factual list of your skills and accomplishments and renewing your own sense of success. Even after you subtract any embellishment, there's plenty left to remind yourself how valuable you are!

10

IDEA Create your "alternative" résumé. Make a list of some of your recent "strength of character" accomplishments that wouldn't be on a normal résumé, and remind yourself why you are a good human being.

For example: You had a difficult interaction with someone and acted maturely by taking the high road; you resisted an "impulse buy" and were responsible about your finances; you graciously passed up the chance to say something bad about someone; you were compassionate and tipped someone well who works hard for their money. Permission to feel good about yourself – granted!

IDEA Focus on what worked and not what didn't. You can always make two lists at the end of the day: Mistakes/Unsolved Problems and Victories/Accomplishments. It's our human nature to make the first list and not the second, leaving us upset and with a sense of imbalance. Catch yourself mentally bemoaning all that you haven't done, or haven't done well, and try going to bed thinking about what you *did* accomplish instead. You'll be more empowered to accomplish things the next day, and you'll sleep better, too.

IDEA Learn to embrace a compliment when you receive one. There's nothing wrong with having strengths as well as weaknesses. Check your response to a compliment: Do you minimize it? Contradict it? Deflect it? How about this – you're allowed to just accept it and relish it. Remember, "Thank you!" is a complete sentence. It feels great to be appreciated. Go with it!

Give Yourself Permission To Feel Good About Yourself

11

Believe In Who You Are

Don't waste time by doubting yourself.

Patricia:

I was about seven years into my professional career as a writer when I made an important transition. I traded my high pressure, no-thanks job at a small advertising agency for the challenges of going freelance. My temp secretarial skills would supplement my writing, and I could hope to enjoy my life again.

Was I a writer if I wasn't being hired to write?

Everything went well for a while, then a slow time as a writer hit and I seemed to be working only as a secretary. I'll never forget what a turning point this was for my self-esteem. Was I a writer if I wasn't being hired to write? I voiced my concerns to my sweet pal Nan, an older, wiser freelancer.

I'll never forget how surprised I was when Nan laced into me with a fair amount of fury. "Don't you ever doubt yourself as a writer when you're between jobs! You are a writer no matter what, just as you are a woman whether you're wearing pants or a skirt. It doesn't come and go; it's who you are. Don't waste your own time and energy by doubting yourself. Get on with it. Shame on you!"

I couldn't go through my life and career with my belief in myself rolling in and out with the unpredictable tides of business.

What Nan said resonated through my being. I reread my résumé and decided she was absolutely right. I couldn't go through my life and career with my belief in myself rolling in and out with the unpredictable tides of business. I was a writer and that was that.

Not only have I never doubted myself again, I've actually delivered the "shame on you" speech a couple of times to younger writers. They seemed as relieved as I had been at the time. Whew! Crisis of self-doubt over...forever!

Accept Yourself Wholeheartedly

12

Allow For Your Worst Day To Become Better

Keep your options – and your attitude – open.

Michael:
Recently, Patricia and I went house hunting in an area we did not know at all. (It's amazing how two intelligent people can start a project like this so foolishly.) I reflect on that day and I don't know how it worked out. And yet it did.

There we were, blindly driving around in a savage rainstorm, barely making out street signs, using a map we couldn't read, with a laptop computer that kept beeping for lack of energy. We even came to a railroad crossing where no train came through, although the lights were blinking and the gate arm was down. I had no patience with this and finally turned the car around. It was just one of those days that seemed symbolized by our being blocked everywhere we went.

It was just one of those days that seemed symbolized by our being blocked everywhere we went.

Miraculously, with only two phone calls from Internet leads, we met with a Realtor who turned out to be knowledgeable, gracious and kind. Riding with her allowed me to sit in the passenger seat, get my bearings and relax. We gained tremendous insight simply by having someone familiar with the area drive us around while telling us stories about the background and nature of the town.

The feeling of the day changed – instead of being disoriented and anxious, I was filled with comfort and hope. And excitement, since we seem to have found a reasonably priced, beautiful area that could lead us to our dream house.

I chose to focus on what worked, not what didn't, and let go of all that frustration.

I felt kind of proud of myself. I chose to focus on what worked, not what didn't, and let go of all that frustration. Doing that allowed the day to transform from being "just one of those days" to being a remarkable one, full of blessings.

Let Things Go Right

13

How Do You Comfort Yourself?

Seth, 28, Personal Trainer

The first thing I do is usually call my parents and my wife. More than likely they have gone through something similar and may have sound advice.

I also scan to a passage in my Bible that will give me wisdom. Many times I can open to a random spot and still find wisdom for the moment.

Every time my heart becomes anxious or worried, I pray rather than letting my thoughts get out of control.

Susan, 55, Realtor/Model

1. Think of the wonderful things in my life and the past joys.
2. Draw cartoons...appreciating the talents I was given.
3. Recall the day I gave birth to my only child and how happy I was.
4. Remember there are those whose lives are much worse than mine and that I will get over it...sooner than later.
5. Light candles throughout my bedroom and turn up classical music.
6. Cry...as much as I want in my own home.
7. Take a long, hot shower.
8. Walk into the woods and sit by the pond.
9. Call my sister, Melanie, an artist.
10. Pray with God and myself.

CREATE 3 ORDER

*Imposing order where there is chaos
gives one an enjoyable sense of hope and empowerment...
though destined to be temporary and revisited!*

MICHAEL BURGOS

It's A Comfort To Turn
Your Piles Of Chaos Into Order

Sift and sort through any messy piles that may be distressing you.

Accumulating things, be they possessions or paperwork, can begin to burden us. Turning the chaos into order gives one clarity and hope.

It's intimidating, though, to know where to start. Like a volcano spewing forth eruptions of lava day after day, our lives fill up with "little mountains" that we begin to overlook or step over. The bigger and messier these mountains grow, the more unapproachable they become. No wonder we become champion procrastinators – we feel overwhelmed!

Undeniably, the disorder in our space feels like disorder in our heads. With chaos as the dominant view, it's actually hard to think straight. Yet, the slightest improvement seems to open the door of possibility . . . to everything.

What do you have to lose? Your room clutter *and* your mind clutter, that's all.

IDEA Use the 15-Minute Rule. You don't have time to start taking apart a mountain – who does? So approach it from a whole different angle: What if you committed only 15 minutes a day to the mess on your desk/floor/nightstand? We love gimmicks, so use a timer and race against the clock. You'll be amazed at how much you can get done in only 15 minutes. And you'll have conquered the hardest part – getting started. (Don't be surprised if you break your deal with yourself and do *another* 15 minutes because you don't want to stop!)

16

IDEA Let someone help you. Just as a mountain climber wouldn't think of scaling a nasty cliff without a partner to spot him, it's smart to tether yourself to someone when approaching what appears to be an uphill task. So grab a trusted friend, spouse or relation and turn the daunting project into a party.

Suggest a trade and help clean up each other's messes, since it's always more fun to go through someone else's stuff. It's also easier to laugh at yourself if you find that lost gas bill from eight months ago when you've got someone to laugh with.

IDEA Clean out your car clutter. Since cars are just rooms with wheels, we probably underestimate how much it affects us to be in the midst of their growing clutter. Get some organizing containers that will carry around your stuff more neatly. A simple trash receptacle in your car will keep it from getting trashy. Schedule a weekly clutter cleanup and notice how much more in control you feel of your whole world. Washing the outside feels like a fresh start, too.

IDEA Play the game "Blessing or Burden?" Pretend you're on a new reality show where someone relentlessly makes you dub each possession from an overflowing closet as a blessing or burden. If it's a blessing, you may keep it *if* you put it where it belongs. If it's a burden, you must either give it away or throw it away – immediately! Remember, the slightest hesitation about whether it's a blessing makes it a burden. Key word: relentless.

Give Orders To Your Stuff

17

Dig Out From Under With The Buddy System

Ask for help when your piles of stuff overwhelm you.

Michael:

Taking control of unruly mountains of stuff is more than a comfort in my own life. As an individual living with ADHD (attention-deficit/hyperactivity disorder), I have found it to be absolutely necessary.

Living with ADHD is like being the perennial absentminded professor. Although I'm vigilant about putting my sunglasses, cell phone and keys with my wallet, hat and appointment book, one of these vital items still manages to go missing from time to time, which just makes me crazy.

As an adult with ADHD, I'm so busy with my thoughts, I can't remember where I put down the glass of water I was drinking just a moment ago. I tend to forget where I put that important paper yesterday that I need now or those duplicate photos I promised to bring someone.

If I had it last week, forget it. And as for last month? It may be lost forever.

...my inability to find what I need when I need it is a source of great anger and distress to me...

I try to be philosophical and say that I never lose things, I just lose track of them (albeit sometimes for a decade); however, the truth is that my inability to find what I need when I need it is a source of great anger and distress to me – and often profound embarrassment.

It got so bad in my thirties that I could have taken the AA oath admitting that I'd lost control of my life – not to alcohol, but to this disorder that creates disorder. It seemed impossible to overcome its effects by myself.

18

So I decided not to do it by myself and learned to use the Buddy System. (I may be unorganized, but I do have the ability to recognize an organized person when I see one.) As a result, I practically keep organized people in my life on permanent retainer. Like my friend Jeanette, who helped me set up my basic filing system with all the same-color plastic tabs one behind the other, since people with ADHD get distracted or frustrated by too many colors or designs.

When she comes over in response to my panicked plea, she scans the cluttered top of my desk and says soothingly, "This isn't so bad." With trepidation, I then point to the three-foot pile of paper under my desk and the six-foot mountain in my closet. She laughs, pats me on the back reassuringly, and digs in while I pace.

Jeanette's presence keeps me calm as we rifle through the piles of unresolved objects and papers. As she uses her skills and objectivity to put everything in its rightful place or create a rightful place, her actions give me a sense of hope. When the chaos has turned into clean surfaces and order, I am filled with a wave of peace.

Knowing that I can find something when I look for it, whether it be my favorite pen, my vitamin C supplement, my black silk shirt or my current credit card bill, gives me a sense of control and empowerment over my own life. For me, that is the greatest comfort that exists.

When the chaos has turned into clean surfaces and order, I am filled with a wave of peace.

Regain Control Over Your Things

19

How Do You Comfort Yourself?

Taylor, 18, College Student
I've come to discover all my kinds of comforts while being away this year.
Here are a few:

Organizing or cleaning	Hugs
A hot, strong shower	Looking at pictures of friends
Lying in bed in total silence	Fall leaves
Wearing a comfy sweatshirt	Coffee

The first snow during the early morning when it is covering the ground
untouched and is balanced on the tree branches

Bob, 51, Financial Consultant
When feeling distressed, the things I do (in addition to the obvious things
such as eating comfort foods, watching TV and going shopping) include:

Rearranging my closets	Making love
Doing fixer-up jobs around the house	Going for a walk
Patting the dog	Doing yoga
Going to the movies	Reading a good book
Taking hot baths	Talking with a friend
Listening to classical music	Answering questions like this one!

CONFIDE YOUR FEELINGS

Feelings that are allowed to fester will kidnap your life

and poison your spirit, body and soul.

Be brave!

Find some way to safely express

your innermost feelings.

PATRICIA ALEXANDER

It's A Comfort To Confide Your Feelings

Release your inner thoughts in a healthy way.

People often add stress to their lives and get stuck by suppressing their feelings, especially if those feelings are uncomfortable ones. This process can take several forms, none of which create any peace.

One of the most common ways to stuff one's emotions is, of course, to stuff oneself. Ahh, the instant oral gratification of food – if only it had no repercussions! Unfortunately, when we're done eating, we're still left with the same unresolved feelings, only now we've added guilt, self-anger and even physical distress from being overfull.

We also commonly ignore our emotions by distracting ourselves with entertainment – the TV, the rented movie, the computer game. Or maybe we just kick the dog and yell at the people we love. All unhappy choices. It may be time to stop treating the symptoms and go after the cause.

IDEA

Write in a journal. What a relief it is to pour your feelings out without interruption or judgment! Journaling can help you in two ways: you get to vent, which is always a relief, and you get to process your feelings so you can move forward. Journaling can also take whatever form fits your feeling – angry words written in slashes or poetry, deep fears you would be nervous to voice out loud, flowery outpourings written with no embarrassment factor.

And once the feeling has been poured out onto the page, sometimes there's an epiphany waiting for you: a revelation that can lead to action or acceptance, either of which will be healthier and feel better than those unexpressed feelings.

22

IDEA → Talk to someone you trust. People tend to feel isolated in whatever they're going through. A sympathetic person you can trust – friend, relative or professional advisor – can say just the right things to help you know you're not alone, and may even be able to brainstorm some real solutions with you.

Not ready for solutions? That's okay – you're allowed to just vent; however, be fair and be up front. Make sure your confidant understands from the beginning that you want a shoulder to cry on, not a solution to try on, so you get what you need and your friend doesn't accidentally make it worse. That's often the result, but never the intention.

IDEA → See a counselor. A trained professional will give you the objective viewpoint you may need in order to work through painful feelings. Think of this person simply as a catalyst to help you figure out important things faster than you could on your own. Money's tight? No excuse – the fee is usually based on a sliding scale. Hard to leave home? Still no excuse – counseling via phone has become even more available. Don't know where to find one? Check your logical resources: church, Yellow Pages, friend, Internet.

Remember: You have the right to choose someone with whom you feel comfortable, and it could take a couple of tries to find a good match. It's well worth it because you're well worth it.

Face Your Feelings . . . So You Can Move On

Let Your Inner Life Out

Pour your thoughts and feelings onto paper.

Patricia:

I was a little girl when I started keeping the classic bubblegum pink Barbie diary, complete with lock and key to keep out pesky siblings. As I evolved, so did my journals – first into spiral notebooks, then into lined, blank, hardbound books.

The journaling process helped me explore the confusion and discoveries of college, the opposite sex, and the ongoing act of reinventing myself. Before long, journaling became a process that had woven its way into the fabric of my life.

I needed to write out my life's events so I could review the complex feelings that came into focus when I put them into words.

Although I had long gaps in my journaling efforts – years when I was too busy or too happy to journal – I returned to it naturally when I hit a pocket of misery in my marriage. I needed to write out my life's events so I could review the complex feelings that came into focus when I put them into words.

As a leader for an international weight loss program, I especially encourage people to journal. I see so many who struggle with high-stress situations and are tempted to comfort themselves with food in a way that only creates more problems.

I assure my groups that writing out their thoughts and feelings comes with no rules, only the opportunity to release their turmoil to a silent confidant who neither interrupts nor judges.

I view my journal as a lifelong cherished companion, trustworthy and ever-present.

My journaling also allows me to count my many blessings while I continue to record the ironies and joys of my still-evolving personhood. As a writer, I love that all of my journals together document my experiences on this earth. I view my journal as a lifelong cherished companion, trustworthy and ever-present.

Discover The Joy Of Journaling

Seek Help When You Hurt

Be open to exploring new ways to heal.

Michael:

After starting to attend a men's group to work through some feelings I was struggling with, I agreed to go to the group's weekend retreat in a mountain cabin. It seemed like an opportunity to get to know a few of the more local guys better in an interesting and meaningful environment.

Our men's retreat leader was a wonderful, evolved therapist with years of experience in guiding men to express their emotions with one another.

One tool he used was to read poems aloud to the group and then invite us to write our own. Although normally reluctant to do this, we were all affected by the ambiance of the dark, woodsy cabin with its crackling fireplace, and the male conclave we had formed. We felt like we were in a safety zone where we could be more open than in our normal nine-to-five concrete-filled environments.

Poems can be playful or serious, lyrical or free-form. However, the poems that came out of these men at this retreat were raw with the pain of broken dreams, unmet goals and shattered relationships. Hard things to talk about and yet, in the guise of verse, this pain found an outlet and a form of comfort.

Personally, I found my poems were all about my mother, who had recently died. They were full of ache and angst, sorrow and grief, all needing to be let out. I was surprised that feelings held so close to my heart could be expressed to strangers, yet the poetry gave me the ability to vent my distinctly private emotions – which is what I needed to begin my healing journey through profound loss.

...the poems that came out of these men at this retreat were raw with the pain of broken dreams, unmet goals and shattered relationships.

I was surprised that feelings held so close to my heart could be expressed to strangers...

Allow Others In To Get Your Feelings Out

25

How Do You Comfort Yourself?

Tayler, 14, Student and Artist
When painting, I get frustrated and just stop doing it. When I feel like this, I go to my teacher for instruction and encouragement. He always helps me realize that if I stick to it, I end up with finished products I really like. That has taught me I have to push through that initial shock of frustration.

Going to people who can encourage me and talking to them about my problems always helps. I find that's true in every aspect of my life, whether it's school, art or even basketball.

Penny, 47, Library Branch Manager, Firefighter, Emergency Medical Technician
My true comfort is in writing. I have kept a journal since high school. It is my companion and my prayer to God. I never leave home without paper and pen.

Russell, 56, Designer
First, I mega-clean my house so every surface shines like new.

Then I call the two people in my life who I know will tell me the absolute truth: my best friend of 30 years and my sister. That way, I get both the male and female viewpoints. I even rely on these two to give me a verbal "smack upside the head," and it's okay, because I know I'm unconditionally loved.

5 ADDRESS REALITY

There will be little rubs and disappointments everywhere,

and we are all apt to expect too much;

but then, if one scheme of happiness fails,

human nature turns to another;

if the first calculation is wrong, we make a second better:

we find comfort somewhere.

JANE AUSTEN
English Novelist
1775 – 1817

It's A Comfort To Stop Fighting Troubles That Won't Change

Solve problems and find peace by addressing reality.

It's our normal human nature to avoid unpleasant experiences, conflicting feelings and unhappy memories. Embracing reality can require that we be "present" with these discomforting situations, not an easy thing to do. In fact, it requires true courage because what we're really tackling is our greatest fears.

Unfortunately, the alternative – refusing to face the truth – can turn into a worse problem. It's not good when our lives and our decisions are run by fear or guilt.

Worst of all, we disempower ourselves from effective problem solving. The result is an inner and outer life of turmoil. Comfort seeking, at that point, can be a matter of taking a weak swing at the symptoms of unhappiness and thus fail to offer any sustaining peace.

That can get old. Be brave, face and embrace reality and take a good, hard *thwack* at the real problem. It may hurt for a while, but you'll hit the home run of your life, feel proud of your courage and receive comfort from the real solutions it brings.

IDEA Catch yourself saying "I should…" "Shoulds" come with very little power except the power to feel guilty. Every time you catch yourself saying "I should…," ask yourself what is the reality of your feelings about the situation. If you can realize and admit that you don't really want to do something and then accept that, you become free to move on to a more empowered perspective that leads to "I will…" or "I can…" Now you're more likely to make it into reality.

28

IDEA → Identify a situation that constantly recurs and accept it. Are you flailing your fists against a brick wall that isn't going anywhere? Your acceptance of that wall as permanent may be the only way you'll figure out how to climb over it.

Ask yourself if there are elements of a situation that probably aren't going to change. If you accepted the situation, what new possibilities would emerge? Sometimes facing reality is the only way you will see a new, creative or viable solution that will bring you peace.

IDEA → Take an action step that you know will be successful. Sit quietly for a few moments and clear your thoughts. Now open your mind to a "worry" thought. What's the first action-oriented solution that pops into your brain?

It might be as simple as communicating to someone what you're thinking or feeling or even allowing someone to brainstorm with you. Or you may need to designate a doable piece of time, say thirty minutes, to spend on making a situation better. Be specific, and choose something you really can and will do. Whatever you come up with will be better than all that unaddressed anxiety!

IDEA → Get an objective opinion. Give someone you trust permission to tell you what they think the reality is that you're too close to see. Perspective from a few steps back can bring a broader view that opens the field for new solutions.

Embrace Reality As A Form Of Problem Solving

29

Accepting Our Human Condition Can Be Empowering

Embrace our undeniable imperfections and work with them!

Patricia:

Ironically, while it is our human condition to be eternally imperfect, we seem to expect perfection from others (some of the time) and from ourselves (most of the time).

As a person who has dealt with weight issues my whole life and who, as a weight loss program leader, has watched other people struggle with their weight issues, I have discovered a potent truth: Even a little acceptance of our human condition goes a long way. Here's a perfect example:

With great looks of guilt, people trying to lose weight often tell me how difficult it is not to eat at night after dinner. Often someone will announce that they have struggled all week and actually managed to conquer their night-eating habits for seven (all right – maybe six) horrible, excruciating evenings in a row. And, yes, maybe they've lost a satisfying amount of weight that week.

But – it could take many months to lose weight. What are the odds they'll stick with it if it's that painful?

The answer is "Not long." We will continue to do only what feels good or has a payoff that's bigger than the former behavior. If we have to give up something that brings us pleasure, the odds are we'll go back to our pleasure source eventually. Again, it's basic human nature. So how about a new approach, one that accepted a behavior we're not likely to give up?

This is where I shock everyone by announcing that the only way I conquered

...I have discovered a potent truth: Even a little acceptance of our human condition goes a long way.

...the only way I conquered my night-eating habit was to give myself permission to continue it.

30

my night-eating habit was to give myself permission to continue it. It brought me a feeling of getting a reward or a treat after a long day and was entertaining. Why would I want to give that up? And once I had accepted the reality that I loved to night munch in front of the TV, I was able to *plan* for it.

I found low-fat, sometimes high-fiber foods that I thoroughly enjoyed, like popcorn, veggies and dip, grapes, ice cream, even lollipops, and munched them in the evening without the slightest guilt. I did that throughout the entire nine months it took me to lose 40 pounds. I still do it.

Could I have lost that weight faster if I hadn't eaten at night? Maybe, but I would have struggled the whole time and felt discouraged whenever I "failed." And I would have failed often, which easily could have driven me to overeat out of shame. I might even have quit the program altogether.

...once I had accepted the reality that I loved to night munch in front of the TV, I was able to plan *for it.*

It was much healthier for me to embrace the reality of being a night eater and then pursue it reasonably – with moderation and without self-recrimination. My body didn't object; I didn't have trouble sleeping, it didn't bother my stomach. It was more about what I ate, not when I ate.

Accepting the inevitability of my need enabled me to problem-solve it from a totally different angle, remain satisfied, and go the distance with my weight loss.

Hey, guys, reality can be our friend!

Make A Situation Better By Accepting It

31

How Do You Comfort Yourself?

Nola, 23, Receptionist for Veterinarian

When I'm feeling stressed out, I enjoy sitting with my husband and dog, just talking and resting. A nice warm bubble bath helps with the tension in my neck and back. Sometimes just vegging out in front of the TV helps soothe the stress from a busy day at work.

Joel, 60, Cartoonist and Animation Artist/Director

I like to work, because my work is my play.

If I've had a day with a lot of stress, I like to sit down, watch TV – the news, if you can believe that – have a glass of wine and kick back. To me that is very relaxing.

If I'm not having a stressful day, I love to putz around in my shop fixing things.

Bill, 72, Retired Pathologist

In general, my philosophy involves first seeing if I can fix the problem that's bothering me. If I can't fix it, I resign myself to the situation and comfort myself by thinking of that old Irish prayer that says "God give me the strength to fix what I can and the wisdom to accept what I can't."

Then I go out in my garden, contemplate the flowers and the beauty of this world and have a glass of wine.

CULTIVATE 6 A HOBBY

A hobby a day keeps the doldrums away.

PHYLLIS MCGINLEY
Pulitzer Prize Poet
Writer of Children's Books
1905 – 1978

It's A Comfort To Cultivate A Hobby

Relieve stress by exploring your interests.

The ups and downs of life on the average human can act like blinders on a racehorse; all we can see is the same circular track, the obstacles in our way and the race at hand. Even if we love our work and our family, we seem to need something else. A hobby!

The dictionary says that to have a hobby is "to have a pastime that you acquire skill at and pursue with the zeal of a child on a rocking 'hobby' horse." So a true hobby expands our abilities and knowledge and engages our passion.

No wonder a hobby often involves our creativity or capability! By its nature, it creates a special area in our life where we can feel excited and personally fulfilled.

What people sometimes forget is that we not only like hobbies, we need them. Obviously, they're effective stressbusters, just by allowing us to focus on something other than work and personal problems. What's less obvious is the way they help us become more interesting people by bringing diversity – and often other hobbyists – into our inner sanctum.

Even a racehorse can run circles inside a big rut; it's the hobby horse, ridden with zeal, that passes it by.

IDEA Go back to a hobby you stopped doing. It's common for people to drop their non-essential interests as their life gets more demanding and their time less available. Think about the things you used to enjoy doing. Do you miss any of them? You might feel more content and have more of yourself to give to your life's demands if you get back to that hobby that interested you.

IDEA Expand your knowledge. Take a class in something that interests you – by yourself or with a friend or relative. (Sometimes we need the partner element for extra courage when doing something new.) What have you always wanted to try? Your local college or your community offers low-cost classes in fascinating subjects, like:

juggling COOKING Singing Acting Calligraphy

GOLF Writing Computers TOASTMASTERS DANCE

Bookbinding Guitar Painting SCULPTURE DRAWING

Improvisational Theatre KNITTING Rubber Stamping

IDEA Think about what interests you and explore further. Are you someone who loves the History Channel? That's a clue that there's a hobby waiting for you. Don't just sit and watch! There are groups that meet to reenact history that are made up of people from all walks of life who love history just as you do. Like to work with your hands? From sophisticated model making to crafts like stained glass or plastic canvas to woodworking, the choices are splendiferous! Wander through a craft or hobby store and see what draws your attention. Do you love Hollywood? Maybe your heart would beat faster to start collecting photos and films of a specific performer or even an animated character. Collectors really enjoy their conventions, and eBay is available day and night.

Give Yourself A Pleasurable Purpose

35

Pick A Hobby You Find Compelling

Allow for a high level of difficulty to keep yourself interested.

Michael:
I have a hobby – or is it an obsession? Hmmm.

Well, there's one thing I know: It's a love/hate relationship and it's with golf.

A good hobby has to be compelling. It's got to be something that draws you intensely. There are four aspects that make golf irresistible to me:

1) Almost all golf courses are aesthetically gorgeous.

2) The joy of spending the entire day out in the sun walking on green grass is far superior to treadmills and noisy, sweaty gyms.

3) Golf is generally played with friends or amazingly friendly people. I have met total strangers at the first tee box and by the end of the day was close to asking them to be in my wedding party! Camaraderie and interpersonal bonding build on a golf course because everyone is dealing with a common enemy – the game itself.

4) Golf is a dramatic game played by passionate people where every stroke is fraught with drama. Will the ball hit a tree and cause you to fight the urge to destroy your own beloved golf clubs or will you achieve the divine ecstasy, that drop of sweet nectar, the beauties of all beauties: the one shot that goes directly to the place you aimed it.

As Winston Churchill said, "Golf is a game whose aim is to hit a very small ball into an even smaller hole, with weapons singularly ill-designed for the purpose."

 That sounds like a great hobby. Or should I say obsession?   Hmmmm.

A good hobby has to be compelling. It's got to be something that draws you intensely.

Golf is a dramatic game played by passionate people where every stroke is fraught with drama.

Develop Patience By Practicing A Hobby

36

Let A Hobby Bring New Things Into Your Life

Remain open to possibilities you wouldn't imagine.

Patricia:

As my 23-year marriage waned down to nothingness, I found tremendous relief from a simple hobby. I began collecting an old TV series from the sixties called *The Adventures of Robin Hood*. I'd had a childhood crush on its star, a dark-haired Englishman with dimples named Richard Greene.

I got thoroughly caught up in Collector's Fever as I played detective, tracking down insider information about the show and its actors. It was so satisfying to find an episode I didn't own, buy it and then run eagerly to the mailbox each day to receive a package sent from anywhere in the world. Soon I was also pursuing photos, merchandise and Greene's movies from the Internet, which I could bid on (a thrilling process) or buy. I went from being an eBay novice to an eBay native.

That's how I met my pen pal. "Robin Hood Ralph" was a married CPA who lived on the Australian island of Tasmania, also seeking relief from stress by collecting the same show! We began chatting via e-mail, sharing links and leads and the fascinating differences of our homelands.

The enthusiasm I brought to my Richard Greene collection helped me get through a rough transitional time in my life. Interestingly, when I met Mr. B., I seemed to lose interest in my dimpled Mr. Greene. Well, not completely. Mr. B. just got many honey points by buying me four new *Robin Hood* episodes.

And if we ever go to Tasmania, I now know someone who would gladly show us around.

Permit A Hobby To Help You Through A Tough Time

As my 23-year marriage waned down to nothingness, I found tremendous relief from a simple hobby.

I went from being an eBay novice to an eBay native.

How Do You Comfort Yourself?

Jeffrey, 14, Student
   I like to turn on the television and watch the Comedy Channel. Laughter is what relieves me from stress.
   I also like to take my mind off the subject and go skateboarding. Skating is great because it takes my mind to a new place.

Cynthia, 35, Weight Watchers Leader and Homemaker
   There are a lot of things I do when I'm distressed:
   • I go to the piano and play because I can get lost in the music.
   • I talk to someone to get it out.
   • I go for a walk to think and just breathe.
   • I also like to read, to take me away.

Cas, 45, Landscape Designer and Contractor
   I like to put myself into a different mental state by putting myself into a different physical state, by taking a walk, going into my greenhouse, breathing deeply, holding my breath, exhaling, trying to bring perspective back into my life.
   I can also remove myself from the current frustration by reading a chapter in my favorite book. If I can't do what I like to do, like fishing, a passion that brings me fulfillment, I read about it – it distracts me in a positive way.

BODY

THE ENTIRE PHYSICAL PART OF A PERSON

Think with the whole body.

ROSHI
Japanese Zen Buddhist Soto Master
1914 – 1982

Courage conquers all things; it even gives strength to the body.

OVID
Roman Poet
43 BC – c.18 AD

The mind's first step to self-awareness must be through the body.

DR. GEORGE SHEEHAN
Cardiologist, Author and Senior Athlete
1918 – 1993

41

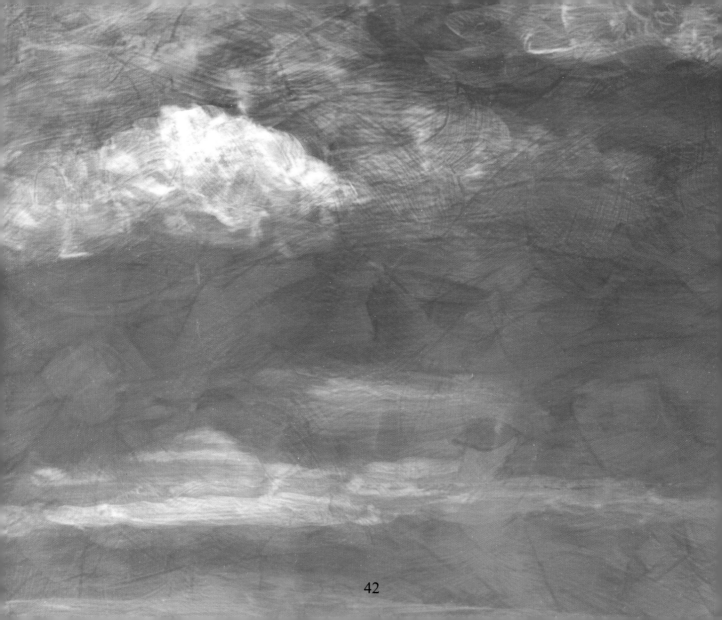

42

7 COMMIT TO SELF-CARE

The person who says

they don't have time to take care of themselves

will soon discover

they're spending all their time being sick.

PATRICIA ALEXANDER

It's A Comfort To Take Care Of Yourself

Parent yourself as you would a real child.

If you had a child who was going from a school day to a sports activity, would you make sure that child had a healthy snack in between? If your child was staying up too late and was tired the next day, would you enforce a healthier bedtime? If your child was spending too much time alone in his/her room, would you set up an outing with peers?

Saying yes to all of these is easy. The harder question is: Would you do the same for yourself?

People are often oddly resistant to taking care of themselves. Sometimes it's a kind of a misplaced guilt, a lie they've accepted that when they look out for their own needs, they're being selfish. Or it's their inner rebel kicking in, refusing an act of adulthood. Perhaps it's about the extra attention they get when they're sick or needy.

In truth, self-caring is an act of kindness to the people we love, because if we're healthy, we have more to give. It is also the most potent act of self-respect – to your body and your personhood. Pursue physical and emotional health simply because you deserve it. And if you think you don't, you have the right to change your mind.

IDEA Anticipate hunger and feed yourself nutritional food. All rationalizations aside, the truth is you usually can anticipate having a crazy/busy day, so have the sense to feed yourself – and make it healthy. Your body is a machine that runs well or poorly depending on the quality and appropriate quantity of fuel it gets. If your engine is stuttering, this is a symptom that you may need a fuel change. A new focus on cause and effect will go a long way to get you farther down the road!

IDEA Get enough sleep. Life's stressful. Sleep is the greatest restorative function of our bodies. Our bodies heal during a good sleep cycle, literally performing cellular repairs. Our brains process the day's events, and our reactions to them, with the necessary outlet of dreams. Give yourself a generous supply of this miracle antidote. Turn off the TV an hour earlier, put on some soft music and go to sleep!

IDEA Move your body. It's so simple, it's true: Use it or lose it. These earthsuits need to move. The good news is you can start from wherever you are and you can do something you enjoy. Start taking vigorous walks by yourself or with a pal. Go dancing or dance in your living room. Try a new activity that interests you, as long as it's active. Your body will thank you with renewed energy and more strength.

IDEA Stay connected with people. Currently, more people live alone than ever in the history of our species. Yet, isolation is poison to our spirits, bodies and souls. We've never been more vulnerable to substituting entertainment for human connection, and electronic communication for face-to-face interaction with human beings.

Spend time with your friends and family. It's an opportunity to enlarge your world, think about someone besides yourself, and stay in balance. If you're short on friends, join a group or class that interests you and ask someone to coffee afterward. Or help your favorite cause with some volunteer work. Now you're in the real world doing real things, living a real life.

Make A Commitment To Healthy Self-Care

Sleep More Often

Take some advice from a feline.

Ender The Cat:

Humans are often awfully irritable. This is, of course, unlike cats, who we all know are mellow most of the time.

Having observed the hectic behavior of humans, I have come to some useful conclusions (not that I expect anyone to pay attention, considering how much people have to be nagged *just* to open a simple sliding glass door for those of us who were not graced with thumbs).

It's simple: To have a better temperament, humans absolutely need more sleep.

I have, however, been graced with insight into what humans are lacking. It's simple: To have a better temperament, humans absolutely need more sleep. They just don't understand what all cats naturally know – that there are many opportunities to sleep and many different kinds of sleep, all quite lovely. Since cats are experts on the subject, and I am of a generous nature, I will happily share my expertise.

...there are many opportunities to sleep and many different kinds of sleep, all quite lovely.

Even humans have recognized the value of the *Cat Nap*, which can be done on almost any corner of a soft bed. That's when cats are in the *Sphinx Pose*, paws straight out in front, head up. This is very calming to the nerves of the royal feline, but humans should not try this pose without the aid of pillows, as their big heads are too heavy.

The *Late Day Nap* is best in a beam of afternoon sunlight. This calls for the *Luxuriating Pose,* where I lie flat on my side, fully stretched out, paws extended, so I can expose my whole body to the sensuous rays of the sun.

Very relaxing.

46

If I'm just in a warm room, I might go into my *Buddha Pose*, with my paws pulled up underneath me. This is a form of self-cuddling, something else cats do well and humans could do better.

And then there's the *Butterball Sleep*, which is the deepest kind. This is where I'm on my side, completely tucked into myself and all you can see is a ball of fur.

While I do sleep at night, I am essentially nocturnal (similar to those of you so attached to that noisy talking box you call the TV). This is when I'm in a hunting mode, so I sleep more lightly, in what we cats call *Meditational Sleep*. In this type of sleep, I may even be sitting up, focusing on sounds and smells, but with my eyes closed.

I think humans often believe if their slumber is not the *Butterball Sleep*, it's not worthwhile. If only they understood the true complexity of the brain (feline or human)!

Cats specialize in accessing different planes of consciousness, as part of the spiritual/physical experience. We see all sleep as a spiritual experience, filled with meaningful visions and completely restorative to our minds and bodies.

I feel sorry for humans, the way they rush around and then sleep so little. No wonder your species is cranky.

I feel sorry for humans, the way they rush around and then sleep so little. No wonder your species is cranky.

Appreciate All the Purrfect Types Of Resting

47

How Do You Comfort Yourself?

Sarah, 23, Aviation Customer Service Representative
1. Sleep. Especially if I am physically exhausted, I like to sleep it off.
2. Be around friends and family, as they usually either get me to temporarily forget my trouble or snap me right out of it (Mom's best at helping me to realize that the glass is half-full).
3. Take a hot shower – it makes me feel revived and renewed.

Cathy, 37, Licensed Massage/Aroma Therapist
I am still amazed after 14 years as a therapist at the power of lavender to calm and bring comfort, or the way vanilla seems to make life seem sweet and uncomplicated. For me aroma is comfort. They go hand in hand.

Marty, 56, Innkeeper/Entrepreneur
The best way to remove stress is to deal with the issue. (A gin and tonic with lime generally takes the edge off very well.) A talk with myself or my wife about the issue that is bothering me often helps to put it in perspective and remove the stress.

Exercise can also change my frame of mind and transform the stressful issue to a conceivable task.

Enjoy Food Wisely 8

The temptation to overeat is like balancing on a fence.

You fall off, say "Ouch!" then hop back on

and try for better balance.

The goal is to stay on the fence a little longer each time.

Patricia Alexander

It's A Comfort To Enjoy Food Wisely

Take solace in satisfying that yen – without negative consequences.

When it comes to instant gratification and quick comfort, food is the obvious winner. It's accessible, affordable and appeasing. It also taps into physical and emotional areas that have depths deeper than chocolate.

It's our genetic disposition to seek comfort food that relates to the weather. There's nothing more relieving on a hot day than an icy drink or an ice-cream cone. If it's cold, then "tuck-in" foods like warm grains and hot beverages feel like a mother's hug.

The most complex need of all is when our emotions drive us to the instant "feel good" of comfort food. It's natural to want to feel better by eating our favorite foods, but the challenge is to stop while it still feels good.

Overeating, which we're all vulnerable to when we're feeling vulnerable, can leave us overfull of food and guilt. You call that comfort?

IDEA Don't think of restaurants as "free" zones. Pleasure becomes pressure when you feel compelled to clean a plate brimming with more food than you can comfortably eat. Order that take-home box with your food and get half of it out of your face right away.

If you butter your toast lightly at home, you can ask for "lightly buttered" at a restaurant. The server wants a tip and the restaurant wants you to come back – so get it the way you want it.

50

IDEA Notice textures as well as tastes. Sometimes we get an urge for something salty-crunchy rather than a specific urge for fat-laden chips. Maybe veggies and dip would satisfy just as easily. Could your desire for pudding have less to do with its sweet flavor than its slippery softness on your tongue? A banana might be strangely satisfying.

IDEA Figure out the reason behind a craving. Sometimes if we actually crave a food, fulfilling that craving is a good idea that's also worth understanding. Are we craving salty foods because we're short on sodium? Dying for chicken because we need protein? Our bodies can be calling out for a vitamin or nutrient that's in short supply. Do some research on any consistent cravings and figure out what your body is trying to tell you.

IDEA Eat comfort foods with wisdom and moderation. Eating an entire box of chocolates if you crave a sweet or cleaning out the pantry at midnight if you're stressed or bored can be a very short-term comfort. Be wise. Try to choose comfort food that comes with limits, like a single-serving bag of microwave popcorn instead of an oversized bag of cheese puffs; an ice-cream sandwich instead of a heaping bowl of ice cream.

Ultimately, you may need to face a problem or deal with an emotion that won't go away with the short-term distraction of food. Be brave – it's worth getting to the source rather than just stuffing the symptom.

Make Food Your Friend, Not Your Foe

Put Food Into Perspective

Be a scientist and observe how food affects your earthsuit.

Patricia:

Growing up in my little family – mother, father and older brother – I was the only overweight person. A reader, not a runner, I felt doomed and soon fell into the classic vicious circle of comforting myself for being fat by eating, often in secret.

It wasn't until I was 19 years old that the strangest eating behavior of all began: I ate because I was hungry, and then I stopped when I was full. I was in love! For the first time in my life, food was not my focus. Rather, I ate until I was satisfied, then looked down at my plate and suddenly realized I'd barely made a dent in the food.

I was in love! For the first time in my life, food was not my focus.

What an incredible scientific discovery! It seemed my five-foot-one-inch medium-boned earthsuit needed only half the fuel of an average adult. That meant that if I ate both halves of a sandwich, it was like filling my tank twice. (Bummer!)

No wonder I was fat. Growing up, I had easily consumed two huge bowls of sugary cereal almost every morning. No one thought anything of it, so why should I? My family ate like any normal household of the late fifties – meat and potatoes with canned vegetables. Fresh fruit. Doughnuts. Ice cream. Candy bars. Normal.

Even though I felt beautiful inside, I would look in a mirror and feel despair.

Even though I felt beautiful inside, I would look in a mirror and feel despair. I spent decades as the poster child for yo-yo dieting, my metabolism eventually lying lifeless at the end of a string of fad diets.

52

Yet when I look at old pictures of myself, I am shocked to see that I don't look fat at all: I just wasn't magazine model thin. I always *felt* fat. What a waste of emotional energy.

However, in my late forties real weight did start to creep on from stress eating while I helped my mom through three cancers. My own menopause did the rest. The most annoying part was that I still ate less than anyone I knew. It just wasn't fair!

As my husband and I were separating, I joined a leading weight loss program with a friend. Ironically, I had to be out of love to remember the science I had learned from being in love: it wasn't about what I ate compared to other people; it was about the total calories needed by this little earthsuit.

The program taught me it was also about a healthier lifestyle. I got more active, discovered I needed (and liked) more water, made healthier food choices. I loved the clear science behind the program's system that allowed me to eat anything, and the flexibility of looking at what I ate over seven days, not one. I got back in touch with what it took to fuel me, not fool me.

After nine months, I dropped 40 pounds, looked 20 years younger, was listening to my body again and was bursting with a renewed excitement for my life. I feel happier being healthier.

I spent decades as the poster child for yo-yo dieting...

...I was listening to my body again and was bursting with a renewed excitement for my life.

Give Yourself Permission To Be Happy

53

How Do You Comfort Yourself?

Mike, 23, Security Guard

Have a snack.
Talk to my friends online.
Call and talk to family.
Listen to music.
Play guitar.

Draw.
Write in my journal.
Go for a walk under the stars.
Talk to myself.
Punch a wall (surprisingly therapeutic).

Neil, 38, Owner/Computer Software Consulting Company

When I was a kid I liked to eat noodles (flat egg noodles), so when I was sick my father made noodles for me as a "feel good" gesture.

More recently, as an adult, I had the opportunity to spend about an hour snorkeling with a pod of dolphins. They were clearly as interested in us as we were in them. Now, when I have a hard time going to sleep, in order to relax, I recall scenes in my mind of those dolphins.

Sandy, 50, Grade-School Teacher

Usually I eat too much, drink too much and watch a lot of TV. That would be pizza, beer and *JAG*.

Though sometimes I ride my bicycle or walk the dog or work in my garden. These are fall back positions if I am out of junk food and wine.

54

SURRENDER TO HEALING

Follow your heartfelt inner voice.
It will lead you to untold miracles of healing.

MICHAEL BURGOS

55

It's A Comfort To Surrender
To The Process Of Healing

Accept the opportunity to become well.

Sometimes there's no use fighting it when you feel ill. If the over-the-counter drugs and vitamin supplements have not stopped the march of germs in your body, you might as well lie down and surrender to the process of being sick…so you can get on with getting well.

Your mind and spirit, if ignored, will also find some way to get your attention, perhaps via a headache or a backache or a serious case of the blues. That's when our bodies are telling us we need to recover from imbalances in our lives.

Even if we're not raging with illness, we may need to stop and give ourselves pause, just to listen to what we really need. Our bodies have recuperative powers – and the word power is no small part of that. Yet it's so easy to take for granted as we grow impatient to get over that cold or flu, to have that broken bone heal or that bruise go away.

Our magnificent bodies are self-repairing machines that yearn for health. Since health is our natural state, our bodies will always tell us what we need to know – that is, if we will listen.

IDEA Listen to your body. If you stop and let your body tell you what is going on, it will reflect the imbalances in your physical form, thoughts and emotions. If your body was a sputtering car, you'd know there was a cause for the sputter. Pain after

56

eating? Your body is telling you about what you ate. Too many colds? Your body wants to tell you that your immune system needs help – are you listening?

IDEA Educate yourself about things that will help your body help itself. Find a health care institution or practitioner you respect and subscribe to their newsletter. Spend some time in a health food store. Read some health-themed books. Cruise some of the health sites on the Internet. There's information out there that might give you new options about increasing your health potential. Your body naturally seeks balance and is eager to heal. Are you aiding that inclination or holding it back?

IDEA Interview the healthiest person you know. If you know someone who seems to be getting it right, maybe they know something you don't. What is it they do to enhance their health? What do they limit? What you don't put into your body can be as important as what you do.

IDEA Let yourself be nurtured. If you feel ill and live with others, let them pamper you. They may even be good at it, if you'll give them a chance. Don't be shy about training them, no matter what you think they should already know. Tell them what you want and need: a glass of orange juice, the shades pulled down, a damp washcloth for your forehead, hot tea and toast, and to be checked on later.

Live alone? Give yourself permission to self-nurture. Get everything you need, cancel your commitments and pour yourself into bed.

Appreciate Your Body's Ability To Heal Itself

57

Listen To Your Body's Requests To Be Healthy

Celebrate your body's natural ability to heal.

Michael:

When I was two years old, I was diagnosed with cancer and had my left kidney removed. I was then subjected to two weeks of intensive radiation therapy. While that successfully treated the cancer, it also seemed to deplete my immune system.

As a child, and then a teenager, I succumbed to dozens of colds, sore throats and flus. Growing up in my family, I can remember hearing my older sister complain to my mother, "Is Mike sick again?"

Neither my family nor I was aware at the time that a diet of McDonald's hamburgers and French fries washed down with Cokes followed by brownies and chocolate-chip cookies were a burden to my body's health. It wasn't until I went to college that I began to become educated about the impact of lifestyle on my number of sick days.

I ate a lot of sprouts and did a lot of yoga in my twenties and felt better for it. I stopped eating red meat and thought tofu in rice and curry sauce tasted better anyway.

Then, when I was 28, I was diagnosed with cancer again. I felt like my body had betrayed me. After some late-life research, I now know that the lymphoma was actually related to the tumor I'd had when I was two, like a double-whammy birth defect.

With the second cancer, however, radiation wasn't enough. I received aggressive chemotherapy treatments for ten months. I can recall being so

When I was two years old, I was diagnosed with cancer and had my left kidney removed.

Then when I was 28, I was diagnosed with cancer again.

58

sensitive to these chemical poisons that I couldn't even drink water for three days after a treatment without throwing it up. Slender by nature, I was eventually reduced to 87 pounds. I didn't think I would ever get well.

But amazingly, 18 years later, I am in better health than I have been in my entire life. Still, the chemo, like the radiation, has left me without the luxury of a robust physical vitality.

If I need to lie down and rest, even in the afternoon, I honor my body's request...

If I need to lie down and rest, even in the afternoon, I honor my body's request for this time to recuperate. I know from experience that if I don't, it could cost me a few days in exhaustion. If I've indulged in coffee, a substance that depletes my immune system, I can become vulnerable to a passerby's cough. If I skip working out at the gym, I can feel my energy seeping away.

I have learned to take better care of myself, mostly through moderation and increased awareness of my physical imbalances. Being acutely sensitive to my body's initial warning signals allows me to make early health interventions. I can't take my health for granted – but then, who really can?

...we have more influence on our health than we realize...or perhaps even appreciate.

Not everyone's a cancer survivor. Certainly, however, we've all caught a nasty cold or had the flu and experienced the great joy and comfort of feeling normal again. It's this miraculous process of healing that reminds us that as long as we live, we have more influence on our health than we realize...or perhaps even appreciate.

Feel Your Own Yearning For Health

59

How Do You Comfort Yourself?

Sean, 36, Concert Promoter
Jacuzzi, television, softball if available, and prayer.

Monique, 43, Banker
First and foremost, I step away and do something for myself, such as soaking in a tub with candles nearby while listening to soothing music. Another thing I do is sit in a relaxing position, breathe and do some yoga movements.

Kathleen, 58, Interior Designer
When I am feeling distressed, I find a way to quiet down my life. Usually going away to silence is most effective for bigger issues. Many times I will use this type of retreat to settle long-standing issues.

When I am not able to go on retreat, a daily sitting of silence helps this process of learning to live more mindfully in every respect. One of the most significant things I have found is leaving the music off in my car.

Another thing that works is to try to do three good things for myself every day that I would usually never do.

GET MORE TOUCH

*Another person's touch brings tenderness to the day
and comfort to the night.*

MICHAEL BURGOS

It's A Comfort To Be Touched

Recognize your human need for hugging and touching.

Skin makes us, by nature, tactile beings. Bursting with nerve endings, skin processes information about our environment, cools our body when we're hot, warns us about dangers, and (thank goodness) gives us enormous pleasure when touched with sensitivity.

Inside that skin is a spirit and a soul that also yearns to be touched with sensitivity. The combination results in a clear fact of nature: We all need to be touched and we all need to be hugged.

It's true that each of us has our own unique touch/hug quotient, determined by culture, family behavior and personal temperament. If that quotient isn't met, however, a person will hit a point of imbalance and fold in on him- or herself, like a flower at night.

The more that people go untouched, the less they blossom. Since this happens slowly over a period of time, the negative effect can either be unnoticed or rationalized to some other cause.

Don't let yourself wither up inside. Touch! Hug! You're only human, and it's our nature.

IDEA Hug and touch people more often (with their permission, of course). Whether you are used to hugging and touching – but aren't doing it lately – or whether your family upbringing didn't include much physical affection, you can deliberately choose to hug and touch more often *now*. In an appropriate way and with inner personal sensitivity, of course. You'll be surprised how receptive some people can be to a quick embrace or a casual shoulder squeeze and how they will respond in kind.

IDEA Pet your pet more often or get a pet to pet. Pet therapy is real, as is witnessed by the many successful programs that bring pets into assisted living residences. Dogs and cats have been good companions for people for ages and the reason is simple: They enjoy being touched and they're a joy to touch. They're soft and warm and respond to the stroking of your hand with pleasing sounds and appreciative glances. Who doesn't need that?

IDEA Book a massage and get rubbed the right way. There's nothing wrong with a good hired hand, and the benefits of body work go deep. The most elemental, of course, is that you're being purposely touched by another human being in a way that feels soothing.

IDEA Get some inanimate snuggle time. Guarantee yourself a calming night's sleep by cuddling up in bed with one of those long body pillows you can wrap your arms and legs around (they can't complain about limbs going dead the way your bedmate can).

Willing to embrace the cute factor? Forget the pillow and get yourself a stuffed animal. Cuddling a stuffie is just as much of a comfort as it was when we were toddlers. A stuffie is soft and huggable, and since it includes the bonus of a personality, you might discover an alter ego that's quite amusing.

Make (Acceptable) Touching A Priority

63

Satisfy Your Touch Needs With A Massage

Hire a professional toucher.

Michael:

I grew up in a family that was very touch-friendly. Both my mother and father gave me abundant physical affection in the form of hugs and kisses, so it follows that as an adult I have always valued cuddle time with a sweetheart.

I grew up in a family that was very touch-friendly…so I have always valued cuddle time with a sweetheart.

At one point, six months after the breakup of a long-term relationship, I found myself growing increasingly touch-needy. It wasn't just the withdrawal from kisses and lovemaking; it was also the absence of human touch and the sweetness that comes from the lingering caress of another human being. As the days/weeks/months went by, I felt an ever increasing ache for this.

I remember that terrible story from an experiment in Russia where babies in an orphanage nursery were not held. They began dying from lack of touch. That's how I felt. It was like going to bed hungry every night – so empty.

Finally, I decided I'd *pay* someone to touch me! Since money was a little tight, I trekked to a massage school instead of a health club or spa. I spoke with the director about setting up a massage with one of the students, sharing with her how much I needed touch because I'd been out of a relationship for so long. I remember she replied curtly, "We don't do that kind of massage here."

Finally, I decided I'd pay *someone to touch me!*

I found myself hurriedly assuring her that I didn't want *that* kind of massage.

Well, it really did help to receive some body work, and shortly after that I met Patricia. But I've never forgotten that feeling of yearning, that empty place, a thirst that could be quenched only by another human being touching me.

Try A Professional Massage

64

Let A Stuffie Into Your Bed

Satisfy your hug quotient in a unique way.

Patricia:

We all need love – agreed? And it feels like love to hold something warm and soft that has some weight to it that we can squeeze and cuddle – agreed?

And doesn't that description perfectly fit a stuffed animal?

No? You'd rather squeeze another human being? Well, sure, that's fine for standing hugs and lovemaking. But I'm talking about hugging all night long as you sleep, and that proves to be highly perilous with humans, who risk the pain of individual parts going uncomfortably numb.

Concerned about the silliness factor? Stuffies are for kids? Exactly! Little ones are comforted for years by clinging to their favorite cuddle toys when left to the angst of falling asleep alone. It's only when they get old enough for pride to kick in that they kick their stuffies out. Well, I've kicked false pride out instead!

My name is Patricia, I am 52 years old and I have slept with a stuffie for over 25 of my adult years.

That said, I'll add that I prefer bears (assuming they pass the hug test). My current bear, Randolph, has been with me for over a decade. He also serves as my grumpy alter ego and provides endless amusement as Mr. B. and I help him come to life and perform what we call "Stuffie Theater."

I firmly believe the world would be a better, more loving and peaceful place if everyone slept with a stuffie. Try it – after all, it's "don't ask, don't tell" – and if you do have a bed partner, they probably won't even notice.

Discover The Secret To The Best Night's Sleep You'll Ever Get

My name is Patricia, I am 52 years old and I have slept with a stuffie for over 25 of my adult years.

Try it – after all, it's "don't ask, don't tell" – and if you do have a bed partner, they probably won't even notice.

How Do You Comfort Yourself?

Shelene, 41, Director of Nonprofit Organization
My kids' belly laughing, butterfly kisses, tickles, getting on my knees and looking into my kids' eyes, heart to heart, eye to eye. (It takes me out of my complicated life and into their innocent sweet life.) A hug from my oldest; a smile from her, too. Life is perfect after that!
Lovemaking! Everything is better after I make love with my husband!

Susie, 42, Wife and Mother of Three
Well, the one thing that comforts me more than anything is being warm. So with that in mind, what really makes me feel good is sitting in the sun, holding and petting my cat, because he seems to have no worries in the world and he can't cause me any harm. In other words, it's emotionally safe territory.

Maura, 49, Personal Productivity Trainer
Sometimes I allow myself to wallow. I take the afternoon off to go to the movies to see a romantic comedy.
Ask my husband for a hug.
Do something nice for someone else. This always works.

11
UNWIND IN WATER

There's no greater comfort
than a hot bath
to drown your troubles.

MICHAEL BURGOS

67

It's A Comfort To Seek Soothing Sensations

Relax in the splash of hydrotherapy.

Sometimes when you feel stressed, the inclination is to drown your troubles in too much food or alcohol. For some people, this can lead to trouble with food or alcohol.

A harmless, inexpensive and easy alternative is to drown your troubles – literally – with hydrotherapy: the comfort of being immersed in water.

Bathing has always been one of life's greatest pleasures because hot water, whether soaking or pounding, soothes and relaxes your body. Even the toughest day seems to wash off under the simple force of water.

Our society seems to know this, as one look at the expanded bath products section of any store will tell you. Soaps of all sizes, scents and colors sit on the shelves next to bath salts, bath bubbles and scrubbing brushes with handsome wooden handles.

One reason we have embraced our sybaritic selves is that hot water also helps you feel enveloped in warmth and safety, just like you were as a baby in your mother's belly. Stressed? Seek out the pleasures of being sent to your womb!

IDEA Take a long, hot, pounding shower. It's almost impossible to feel weighed down with problems under the stream of a soothing, massaging, pulsating shower. Soaping up and rubbing your skin with a washcloth or loofa sponge miraculously seems to cleanse the mind as well as the body, and allows you to emerge with a clean perspective. Try showering in the dark or by candlelight – it's a whole new experience, with emphasis on luxuriating, not exfoliating.

68

IDEA → Take a swim. Moving in water touches our senses like nothing else. We trade our heavy earth bodies for more buoyant water bodies. We also feel the softness of water, silky and fluid against our skin. Make time to go swimming in your local lake or ocean; seek out a swimming pool, cold or warm, and glide through the water with strength and grace. It's utterly renewing . . . especially if you can leave your bathing suit behind!

IDEA → Get thee to a Jacuzzi. You might have to make some arrangements with some friends, pay a day fee at a hotel, gym or spa – or maybe just make it a priority to actually use your own Jacuzzi – but you'll be grateful you did. Tubbing in hot water with jets takes the body to a whole new level of relief. Pressured water vibrating against your muscles acts like a tranquilizer shooting through your being. You knew this, you just forgot.

IDEA → Take a bath with the works. Turn your bathtub into a comfort zone by adding mineral salts, bubbles, oil, incense and an inflated back pillow. Flick off the fluorescents, light up some candles, and put on your favorite music. Most women know that a good soak in the tub will float away the annoyances of the day.

Men: Tubs are underused by you because you're too long for them. But not all tubs are equal. When you get access to a bigger than normal tub, consider giving it a try – you may like being in hot water more than you know.

Unwind In Water

69

Let Your Shower And Tub Ease Your Pain

Take relief where you can find it.

Michael:

When I was 28, I underwent six months of chemotherapy for a lymphoma that had made an unwelcome home in my youthful body. My sensitive system didn't take well to these "smart" poisons, and soon I found myself experiencing constant gastrointestinal distress.

Since pain medication inflamed my digestion even further, I had to look for alternative ways to comfort myself. Fortunately, my shower-tub turned out to be a place of true relief. In fact, often all I could look forward to was the soothing heat of a hot shower.

...often all I could look forward to was the soothing heat of a hot shower.

These showers evolved into baths as the chemotherapy weakened me to the point where I could only start off with a shower. As my strength drained away, I would lie down and let the water pour onto me from above, finally just turning it into a tub.

Seventeen years later, I thank God I am cancer-free. This habit of seeking comfort in both a shower and a tub has stayed with me. I carry into my current life a strong association with the relief water brings from a time when there was very little comfort to be found. And I really do still enjoy just taking a sit-down in the shower and letting the water pour over me. It's an odd comfort technique born of distress and pain, yet carried forth with good cheer into better times.

And Patricia can testify that I'm the cleanest man she knows – even if there's no hot water left for her!

Take Pleasure In Water Works

70

Drench, Splash And Soak Your Stress Away

Get creative with your water ways.

Patricia:

Michael says I have raised the bathtub experience to an art form. In spite of the fact he is one of the few men I know who appreciates a steamy bath, he still approaches it in its most pure form – a tub of water. Since the basic bath has brought him so much relief over the years, it's been especially delightful to introduce him to some embellishments.

Like many women, I have taken the bathtub experience to its most luxurious extreme. I am overjoyed when a blanket of thick, lavender-scented bubbles covers me completely. And it can – because I own ingenious drain blockers that let the water rise dangerously high.

...I own ingenious drain blockers that let the water rise dangerously high.

I like the water really hot and the nearby glass of wine really cold. Some jazzy music floats my mind away from anything stressful, and candles turn the darkened room into a palace. I sigh and lean back – I'm in little princess heaven. My standards for a bathtub are high, however. If the tub is shallow or poorly shaped to torture the neck, I'd just as soon skip it and become Shower Girl.

I like the water really hot and the nearby glass of wine really cold.

Showers are an instant vacation, with the word "relax" pulsating from the showerhead. (Devices that limit water pressure are the work of the devil.) Scented soaps are a must, as is body oil you can squirt right onto your skin.

Best of all, showers allow me to start the water reasonably warm, then slowly turn up the heat all the way to volcanic. My bones disappear, my muscles release their stress grip and life becomes a beautiful thing.

When Life Gets Tough, Get Wet!

71

How Do You Comfort Yourself?

Erin, 27, Fitness/Wellness Specialist
Take a hot bath or shower.
Cry.
Have a bowl of soup or Top Ramen.
Call a friend or family member.
Cuddle with my boyfriend.
Watch a movie.
Curl up with a book.
Exercise (all types).
Shop.
Drink a glass of red wine.
Get a manicure and pedicure.
Listen to loud music in my car and sing very loud or even scream.

Primus, 28, Computer Game Tester
When I feel distressed, I like to take a shower because it is a way to set aside a length of time during which I know I won't have any problems to deal with. If I take a bath, I can hear the phone ring or someone might knock on the door and yell a question for me. If I am taking a shower, everything waits until that is done. Of course, it also helps that hot water massages my neck and back.

Phyllis, 50, Receptionist
When I am distressed, I take a long walk. It always clears the cobwebs and helps me to get things in perspective.
A long relaxing bath with candles follows. It is a definite de-stressor!

RENEW YOUR CONNECTION WITH THE EARTH

Keep close to Nature's heart . . .

and break clear away, once in a while,

and climb a mountain or spend a week in the woods.

Wash your spirit clean.

JOHN MUIR
American Naturalist
1838 – 1914

It's A Comfort To Renew
Your Connection With The Earth

Go find yourself a piece of nature.

It's so easy not to remember that the world wasn't created with the stress our modern life brings with it, surrounding us with buildings, traffic and constant sound. No wonder we forget the degree of comfort that can be brought by going back to our Mother – Mother Earth.

If you can, go someplace where there is only nature. You will hear a strange sound: the lack of civilized noise. Nature is not silent, though. There will be sound to which your ears may have grown deaf. Listen to the wind rustling in the greenery, the strange clicks and hums of the insects, the air swooshing from the wings of a bird.

Now bring your other senses to the surface. Rest your eyes on silky green grass. Run your hands over the gnarled roughness of tree bark. Smell the dark goodness of soil and the spiciness of plants. Tune in to the natural energy of the earth pulsating with life for everything that grows.

Yes, that's right – you're not in a building anymore!

IDEA Familiarize yourself with your national, state, county and city parks. Deliberately seek out the nature that's available to you, compliments of your government. You may be surprised at how reasonable a drive it is to some of the best-kept and most diverse pockets of natural beauty. Make it a mission to seek out every park on your home turf. You'll be surprised at the peaceful little Edens that exist whether you take advantage of them or not.

Did you know the national parks have a free, fun and informative book they call a "Passport" where you can collect stamps for each park visited? Now that's a great hobby!

IDEA Take a hike on a nature trail. Check your local paper for easy hikes led by a guide who will tell you all about the local birds, flowers and animal life. Remind your feet what it feels like to walk on the uneven earth instead of the monotone of pavement. Hiking on this good earth is much more interesting than that exercise bike, anyway, and still counts as exercise.

IDEA Go for a stroll near water. If you live near an ocean, lake or river, when was the last time you sat down next to it and just watched the movement of the water? No water nearby? How about a park or condo complex with a stream or pond? Even in the midst of urban sprawl, you can find buildings with man-made waterfalls or lovely fountains.

IDEA Find a place of nature in an unnatural place. Four-star hotels with accessible lobbies can be a great source of architecturally enhanced nature, often full of lush plants and beautiful water structures.

Do you have a home without a yard? Bring some plants onto even the smallest balcony or porch and turn it into a nature-lush place to sit. Catch a moment in a sunbeam and close your eyes. Has the world shrunk…or expanded?

Rest In The Arms Of Mother Nature

75

Bliss Out With Some Sunlight

Stop and feel a natural pleasure.

Michael:

Recently after computer gaming for 14 straight hours, blurry-eyed and experiencing tendonitis in my clicker finger, I looked up and noticed our cat, Ender, sprawled on the patio, right in a sunbeam. You could see that he was relaxing into the comfort of the natural warmth shining down on him. It stopped me – he was the picture of bliss.

Sensing that by his animal nature he knew a good thing (that might be missed by us overcomplicated humans), I drew myself out of my dimly lit male cave and forced myself into the light where my wise feline friend had found a simple pleasure.

My mind dropped all its worries and embraced the full joy of a few minutes of warm, natural sunlight.

In fact, I lay down next to him, taking off my shirt and draping it over my head, soaking up the beneficence that spreads its goodwill to all of us on sunny days. Then I closed my eyes, feeling safe, warm and tranquil.

I didn't stay long, no more than ten minutes. But in that time I swear I could feel the vitamin D forming in my body. I could feel the sun's heat relaxing both my back and my muscles as I mimicked Ender's luxurious stretches.

My mind dropped all its worries and embraced the full joy of a few minutes of warm, natural sunlight. I arose refreshed and slowed down. I've learned to trust my animal friends for their instinct for comfort and for their absolute disinterest in any information or entertainment that comes through a glowing blue screen.

Sometimes it takes the wisdom of a family pet to lead us to a small comfort.

Give Yourself A Moment In The Sun

76

Let Your Feet Touch The Earth

Get out from being inside.

Patricia:
I have never been athletic or outdoorsy. I camped a few times in my youth, but thought of it quite literally as the last resort. Falling off my bicycle when I was ten took bicycling firmly out of the realm of fun. And jogging rhymes with flogging for good reason as far as I can tell.

So it is a great surprise at the fifth decade of my life to find myself wearing an outdoorsy-looking outfit, complete with cap, boots, backpack and water bottle. It is a bigger surprise to discover I am actually enjoying myself while doing something as athletic-sounding as hiking.

I owe it all to my Mr. B., who is one of those rare people who cannot tread cement for too long without instinctively seeking an uneven dirt path to explore. By happily tagging along on his adventures, I have seen breathtaking views that were not outside my window, touched a wall of moss as it grew like a carpet next to a waterfall, and smelled the fresh earth vibrating with new life after a rainfall.

One time we sat on a thicket of needles under a giant redwood for about 20 minutes and just listened to the forest. We stayed so still, little lizards skittered by us as if we were rocks. We got to eavesdrop on the birds and squirrels, who settled back into their conversations as though we interlopers had moved on.

There is a vital part of my soul that is fed by these outings, a part I had been neglecting for too long. I may be connected to the computer and the TV and the telephone – but, lest I forget, I am also of the earth.

There is a vital part of my soul that is fed by these outings, a part I had been neglecting for too long.

...lest I forget, I am also of the earth.

Rediscover Your Outdoor Roots

77

How Do You Comfort Yourself?

Lisa, 47, Vice President/Cleaning Service
I walk along the beach, dig my toes in the sand and watch the waves.

Barbara, 48, Librarian
There are two places I have consistently sought and found to be very comforting when I am distressed.

The first is outdoors. To feel the fresh air and focus on the life going on outside of the human realm: the plants, trees, insects, birds, landscapes, waterways; to observe the weather, the celestial marvels; to see the unique beauty and power that moves through the natural world, and remember there is much more to this amazing planet than human drama.

The other is inside a good book. Reading can give me a break from my own issues and give me a chance to reapproach my emotions in a more indirect manner while enjoying another's artistry and insight.

Charles, 54, Clinical Psychologist
I do one or more of several things: go for a walk, preferably in nature, talk with close friends who are a part of my support system, write in my journal, listen to music, do yoga.

Social contact, being with other people, having dinner or going to cultural events also can relieve my distress.

SOUL

THE VITAL ESSENCE OR HEART OF A PERSON; THE ANIMATING, INDIVIDUAL FORCE OF A HUMAN BEING, OFTEN BELIEVED TO SURVIVE DEATH

Man can never be happy
if he does not nourish his soul
as he does his body.

UNKNOWN

The soul, like the body, lives by what it feeds on.

JOSIAH GILBERT HOLLAND
American Editor and Writer
1819 – 1881

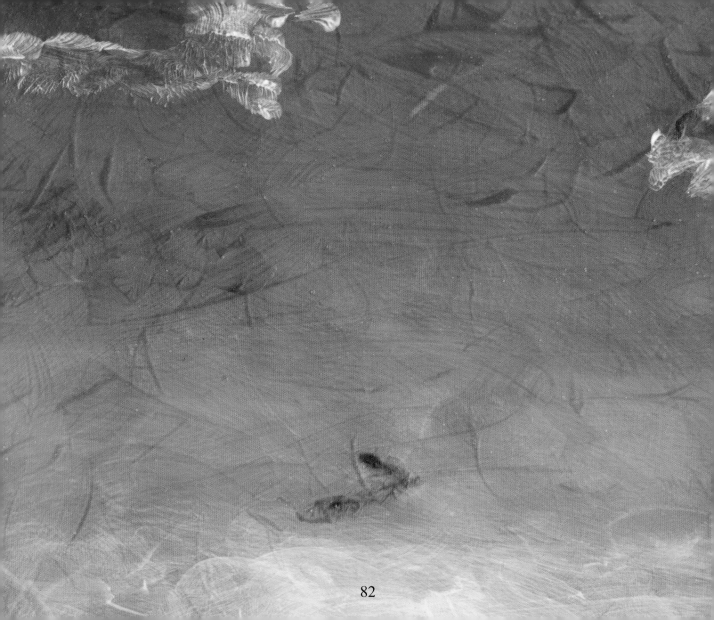

82

13
KNOW WHERE TO TURN

Sometimes I hold you up;
sometimes you hold me up.
Since every single one of us will stumble,
it's a comfort to go hand in hand.

PATRICIA ALEXANDER

It's A Comfort to Know Where to Turn For Instant Calming

Think about where you'd go first.

Someone you trust betrays you . . . you are fired . . . you have an accident . . . someone you love dies. These are the sudden and emotionally powerful dramas of life that hit us in our soul and our gut. The need to seek comfort at these times is a primal reaction, as embedded in our DNA as the fight-or-flight instinct.

The first comforts people think of may include alcohol, drugs, too much food or marathon sleeping. However, since these all have dire consequences, their ability to comfort is short-term. In the end, we feel worse than when we started.

We have to think ahead, because it can help to know the answer before a life-changing event makes it hard to think. Knowing where to go, whom to talk to, or whom to reach for after an earth-shattering shock can provide the kind of comfort that runs deep.

So ask yourself: Where can you go when you're in crisis?

IDEA Identify the person with the voice or hug you crave. After bad news, there's nothing like hearing the steadying voice of a loved one, so much so that their actual words may not come through until later. A warm, lingering hug is even better, whether from mother, mate or pal. Sometimes human touch – the laying on of hands – can impact our pain even when it can't solve our problems.

IDEA Go where everyone knows your name. A local hangout filled with familiar faces – whether it's a church, bookstore, coffeehouse or diner – can bring the relief of the familiar. We can be sitting all alone, still in shock, yet feel soothed to be surrounded by the world's continuing rituals. It gives us hope that our world will get back to normal, too.

IDEA Go to beauty and safety. Certain physical environments are balms to our hurting souls. We are drawn to the ocean or a breathtaking view, a favorite oak, a quiet place in the park, a garden, the night sky, a fireplace...

Only you know the place that calls to you when you hurt desperately. You might be surprised that it's nothing more exotic than the big comfy chair in the corner where you can sink into yourself to reflect in peace.

IDEA Take to your bed. For some, there's no higher comfort than sending yourself to your figurative womb – your bed. Shutting down is the body's and mind's safety valve for shock. There's nothing wrong with this in the short term – so long as it doesn't turn into self-defeating denial or ongoing depression. Give yourself permission to retreat and regroup. A hug from your bed amid the safety of soft sheets, plump pillows and warm blankies can be restorative.

IDEA Pray. Whatever your belief system, a crisis reminds us that we are spiritual beings. Instinctively, we find comfort in calling on a greater power to which we can release our fears and pain while we seek a deeper understanding. There is peace here. Ask and you shall receive.

Seek Your Safe Place When Life Falls In On You

85

Value The Things That Comfort Your Soul

Know you are connected to people, places and powers.

Patricia:
When I think of the most unsettling moments in my life – and believe me, I know I've been fortunate to have so few – I think of how they have drawn me to the people I love and trust, as well as to special places.

I see myself at 21, when my college marriage collapsed, talking through the night with my sweet, supportive mother, who listened to me intently while stroking my hand.

...I was on the verge of a nervous breakdown from a job that was grinding me to dust.

I see myself at 23, being gently bundled out of my workplace late at night by my best friend, who came to get me when I was on the verge of a nervous breakdown from a job that was grinding me to dust.

I see myself at 27, sobbing in my second husband's arms at his office while he waved people away. I had driven straight to him after finding the grisly remains of our beloved cat, who had been killed by a coyote.

I see myself at 29, walking on the beach holding hands with my husband in a somber get-away weekend, prior to having a surgery that was thought to reveal a cancer that could keep me from bearing children. Thankfully, it was not cancer and I was soon pregnant with my only child, our son.

I see myself at 34, calling a prayer line after my husband went ballistic in a restaurant. He soon confessed to having a hidden drinking problem and began trying to manage it.

I see myself at 46, clinging to the warm voice of my loving brother over the phone in my mother's room at an assisted living residence, where I had just witnessed her peaceful death.

I see all five-foot-one of me at 48, after having caused a minor three-car accident, being lovingly swept into the comforting bear hug of my six-foot-one son, as I wept with remorse. It was the day before Christmas.

I see myself at 52, emerging from the car in our garage and straight into the haven of Mr. B.'s waiting arms, as I returned from a tense three-day hospital experience, acting as protector/advocate for my dear 75-year-old friend and mentor.

I also remember highly emotional moments when I felt deeply hurt by people and sought comfort in places. Once I walked for miles up and down a beach, talking to myself, pouring my despair into the vastness of the waves. And one time, when I could not figure out where to go after a huge fight with my husband, I was surprised to end up at the library, drawn by the steadfastness of the books, my old friends.

Churches have also been a place of deep comfort for me. I remember crucial times of intense anxiety, when I prayed, alone or with others. When I opened myself up to connect with my spiritual source, I received a peace that went beyond any understanding.

For all these moments of comfort, I am grateful.

I remember highly emotional moments when I felt deeply hurt by people and sought comfort in places.

When I opened myself up to connect with my spiritual source, I received a peace that went beyond any understanding.

Go Find What You Need

87

How Do You Comfort Yourself?

Erin, 26, Bed and Breakfast Manager
In most cases, nothing feels better than sharing my problems and concerns with my wonderful husband. It just feels good to "get it out" and then, together, work to solve any confronting issue.

Linda, 46, Quality Assurance Manager
For *emotional* distress: My first inclination is to call my mother (I am so lucky to still have her to call). I also take a hot bath, read a good book, pray or go visit a close friend. However, I also still revert to eating sweets, ice cream and the foods that have always comforted me.
For *physical* distress: I also call my mother – she's an RN – I pray, or go to bed (I love to sleep, only it gets harder the older we get).

Gary, 52, Photographer
Slow, deep breath "God is" on the exhale and "I am" on the inhale. Works every time.

14
ACT WITH SELF-COMPASSION

Self-compassion is not about losing your inner critic;
it's about transforming it
from a bitter, self-destructive voice
to one tempered with humor and forgiveness.

MICHAEL BURGOS

It's A Comfort To Combine Action With Self-Compassion

Get out of "guilt-jail" free.

You don't have to commit a crime or break a law to be found guilty in the court of your own mind. Deserved or not, we often convict ourselves of felonies that sentence us to days, weeks, months – even years – of self-punishing feelings of guilt. And as with anything that involves procrastination, the longer you let it continue, the worse it feels.

We're so hard on ourselves! It's amazing the kindness we would instantly offer to loved ones, or even complete strangers, that we would not give to ourselves. There's danger in it, too. Our personal growth can get stuck in place if we do not allow ourselves to acquire the art and wisdom of self-forgiveness.

Guilt is also terribly counterproductive. We humans have a funny habit of lashing out at those who make us feel guilty, making everything worse. If we're making ourselves feel guilty, we're either going to seek self-punishment – very unhealthy – or hide from our bad feelings. That's classic denial – also not productive, also unhealthy.

You don't have to live this way. Give yourself a chance to address your guilty feelings in a healthy manner – and breathe a sigh of relief.

IDEA Make a literal Guilt List of everything that's haunting you. It could be as mundane as having put off a chore way too long or as serious as having said something hurtful to someone you care about. It's time to get all the guilts, small and large, out of your head and down on paper. Take a look at what it would really take for you to walk around guilt-free.

90

IDEA → Address something on your Guilt List each week. If it's a task, do it. If it's an apologetic note, write it. If it's an overdue phone call, make it. Now get yourself a jumbo black marker, and as you clear up the things on your list, cross them out with a big, satisfying, eradicating black sweep. Ahhh, what a pleasure – and what liberation!

IDEA → Keep your inner voice on high volume. One of the things about mistakes is that they seemed like a good idea at the time. If we thought it was going to be a mistake when we did it, we wouldn't have done it! So most of the time, it's not until after we've done it or said it or neglected to do it that the little instinct inside of us makes noise. Once that inner voice in your head starts whispering, it's your level of awareness that determines whether it goes away or goes louder. So keep your inner voice on high volume and catch your mistakes more quickly all the time. End result: no new guilt.

IDEA → Present yourself with an official pardon. We've all made mistakes and misjudgments – we're human. Once you've done all you can do to rectify the undone of the past, the next step is to forgive yourself and let it go. Doing this is easier if you reframe your guilt from a negative into a positive by having learned something that you'll apply to the future. Now you're a better person. Being punitive is pointless – go and sin no more!

Present Yourself With A Pardon

91

Lighten Your Emotional Load

Tackle the top two things on your Guilt List.

Patricia:

It's a normal day and I'm responding to the tyranny of the urgent: keeping appointments and promises, cheerfully running the necessary obstacle course of life (market, bank, post office).

Suddenly I am aware of an oppressive feeling. Despite being productive, I'm feeling guilty. What is it?

Despite being productive, I'm feeling guilty. What is it?

Mentally, I reach into the recesses of my mind for my Guilt List. Uh-oh! It's grown. No wonder I can feel it – it's seeping out of the corners! I sigh. No more avoidance – I'd better take a look.

Oh, there's that press release I said I'd write a week ago for my favorite nonprofit charity. Oh, and I meant to call my girlfriend who's just left her husband and make sure she's okay – I'm ashamed I let that go.

Mentally, I reach into the recesses of my mind for my Guilt List. Uh-oh! It's grown.

I know if I don't clean up my office very, very soon, I'm going to doom myself to losing something very, very important. And there's more. (Feeling overwhelmed now.)

I look at my watch. I've got time to do the top two. Do I have the energy?

I think about how much energy it will take to carry this oppressive feeling around another day. My priorities just changed and I'm headed to the computer and the phone. Whew! I feel better already.

Of course, that means the messy office just rose to the top of the Guilt List. Oddly enough, that gives me hope.

Feel Better About Yourself By Doing What You Can Do

92

Identify Your Patterns Without Being Judgmental

Give yourself permission to be human.

Michael:

This information revolution we're in always makes me think there are so many great things we can do. Yet, rather than inspire me, these boundless options and opportunities seem to contribute to my personal Guilt List.

As it turns out, unlimited potential – my own and the world's – is sometimes a stalling point. Everything that I want to do overwhelms me. My Guilt List is littered with the "shoulds" and "ought tos" of unaddressed potential. Thankfully, I recognize that I have an established pattern for resolving these frustrating feelings.

My process is to whittle all my opportunities from a giant plank of worry into a walking stick of action (eventually). In this process, I accept that I wield this "walking stick" like…um, well…a weapon.

That is, I usually tackle Guilt Lists with explosions of anger that create a flurry of activity. When the explosion is over, however, I have ended up taking small, tangible steps toward bigger goals.

And as long as I don't break anything valuable, this burst of energy is helpful and moves me through my stuck place of anxiety to a more comfortable place of progress.

As it is with many men, anger seems to create the energy that moves me forward. Not the perfect process – but a process nonetheless.

I usually tackle Guilt Lists with explosions of anger that create a flurry of activity.

…anger seems to create the energy that moves me forward. Not the perfect process – but a process nonetheless.

Accept Your Own Process For Dealing With Guilt

93

How Do You Comfort Yourself?

T.J., 21, College Student

I find that turning to music is often a fulfilling way to unwind. Music is powerful. It is most pleasurable to become enveloped in my choices and eliminate outside distractions, whether via headphones or surround-sound audio.

If you are passionate about what you're listening to, you can become lost in it, whether it be a Kronos Quartet symphony or punk rock by Green Day. (Also, as a typical college student, I further recommend a drink or three containing quality chilled beverages to complement whatever melody you select.)

Terry, 51, Business Developer

Comforting myself drops in relation to a proactive or reactive response and whether I feel I have already tried to deal rationally with the issue. I also:
1) Seek new solutions/ideas and revise my game plan (intellectualize).
2) Call/see a friend who loves me . . . be with or talk to people.
3) Go shopping (depending on fund availability).
4) Cry, if it is creating sadness.
5) Write (poetry, short stories, etc.).
6) Pray (unfortunately, only when extremely low).

Eric, 52, Executive

Perhaps you have just identified my problem.

94

15
SCHEDULE ALONE TIME

Being comfortable in your own skin

and content with your own company

is a magical gift

to yourself and everyone in your life.

PATRICIA ALEXANDER

It's A Comfort To Schedule Some Ritualized Alone Time

Renew your spirit and soul a little bit more often.

If your life is drop-dead busy and you'd like some peace and quiet, the odds are you're not going to get it by accident. You might rationalize that driving alone and doing chores by yourself is alone time, but it's not. Restorative alone time usually has to be scheduled.

Whether you're craving quality alone time or not, it could be exactly what you need. Responding to others, hearing them, seeing them – all takes up space in your spirit.

If you start scheduling alone time, you'll observe an interesting result: a more balanced sense of inner self and greater personal serenity. Now watch the positive trickle-down effect on everyone with whom you come into contact, blessing you and those you love.

IDEA   Go out to breakfast or lunch with your favorite thing to read. Tired of being interrupted while you're trying to read the sports page or the entertainment section? Leave the house with the newspaper or magazine of your choice and eat the meal you'd eat anyway, with the printed word as your companion. (And turn off that cell phone for an hour – you'll get your messages when you're done.)

IDEA   Get up a little earlier before you or your household normally starts the day. Sometimes the only way to put something in "Column A" is to take it from "Column B." If your schedule won't relinquish any "you" time, consider giving up some sleep. When you start the day with quiet morning time, you'll discern a subtle difference in how you handle the day's challenges. Read a book or newspaper,

96

write in your journal, listen to music, do crossword puzzles, do some extra bathing or grooming. Your ability to handle everything in your day will improve!

IDEA Schedule some meditative strolls. Our noble quest for fitness has turned our walks into fat-burning exercises. Start going for a daily meditative stroll by yourself where you get to notice the texture of the trees and feel the air on your face – and leave your pedometer at home.

IDEA Design the perfect "me" day or weekend at least once a quarter. Think what a joy it would be to have an entire day or weekend of freedom in a new setting. This is not as hard or as expensive as you think. Seek out retreat centers that are within a drivable distance. These can vary from spa to spiritual and probably have one-day or short-stay rates that are well worth it.

Take yourself to the movies. Stroll through that museum you've always meant to visit. Drive a few hours to a different terrain: beach, mountains or desert, whatever's different from what you see all the time. Give yourself some spending money and go to the mall by yourself without having to rush or run errands. Sit in a park and watch children play and dogs romp.

The result will be that you'll reexperience your more centered self, renew your creative self and come back with more real self to give your real world.

Give Yourself Some Peace And Quiet On Purpose

97

Create The Peace And Quiet You Need

Give yourself the gift of some quality alone time.

Patricia:

Long ago, when I was a freelance writer, a wife, and a mother to a growing boy, I discovered something important: I really hated to start each day by hitting the ground running. If my morning slammed me into action immediately, I felt like I was chasing time all day and never catching up. It was nerve-racking.

One morning, I did something different. I set my alarm for 30 minutes before our little household had to be up. I made myself a cup of coffee, put on some jazzy music, sprawled on the couch and read a book, relishing that I was the only one awake in a quiet house.

I soon realized I had more to give my family and my work if I could start each day with this time to myself.

Ahhh! That was better. I soon realized I had more to give my family and my work if I could start each day with this time to myself.

Now, although my child is grown and I have a different mate, I still savor that 30 minutes of alone time as my springboard into the day. My Mr. B. and I have a system where, if I have to get up earlier than he does, he slips off in the middle of the night to our second bedroom so he can sleep in and I don't have to tiptoe around as I get ready.

But before I get ready, I get to stay in bed for my special quiet time. I turn on the cable music channel, going for jazz if I have to rouse myself to a busy day, something quieter if I'm groggy-headed from lingering dreams. I sip the cup of coffee I've made myself (ambrosia!) and munch a toasted bagel.

98

As I do this, I lean back into a pile of pillows that generate a comforting surge of warmth that flows through me like a heating pad. My cat, Valentine, Ender's sister, curls into the curve of my waist, her front paws on top of me as though holding me down. (Okay, she is holding me down – this is her favorite time, too.)

To me, the ideal morning is when I can use this time to do this and all my favorite quiet-time things. I read my current book of fiction, then a few pages of something nonfiction. I write in my personal journal so I can process important feelings and events. I write out a blessing for the Blessing Box. I may even do my nails.

Sometimes, as a special treat, I work on a crostic, a type of puzzle more interesting to me than a crossword. I usually only get to do these on vacations, so doing a crostic at home gives me the delicious illusion of being on vacation.

Checking the clock, I sigh and yawn. Time to get up. Boy, that 30 minutes flies by! I often sneak an extra 10 minutes, though it's a rare and guilty pleasure if I can rationalize a whole hour. I gently displace Valentine, who communicates her annoyance with a cat sound that "meow" doesn't describe. I stretch my arms wide and reluctantly leave my warm, protective pocket of covers and pillows.

Starting as I have, slowly and sweetly, I feel refreshed, infused with energy and ready to take on the challenges of the day.

Starting as I have, slowly and sweetly, I feel refreshed, infused with energy and ready to take on the challenges of the day.

Make Time For Yourself

99

How Do You Comfort Yourself?

Bob, 46, Community College Instructor
Hot fudge sundaes and long, slow drives on a country road.
Anything out of my ordinary schedule helps me reframe my own borders and puts things into perspective.

Sona, 51, Freelance Book Editor
I will watch old movies (from 1931 to 1949), since they soothe me, are non-threatening, and require nothing back from me.
I will eat, although I'm disciplined enough by now not to eat high-calorie foods, I will eat low-calorie foods in volume (cabbage, broccoli, Brussels sprouts), essentially to stuff myself into not having to feel whatever is bothering me.
And I will want to be alone, so that I won't have to engage outside myself with others (that takes too much energy, at a time when I am in need of replenishing my energy). I won't necessarily need to take myself to someplace bucolic – my own apartment in the city is fine – but if I am at my cabin, I will enjoy gazing at the serenity all around me.

16
Choose Your Attitude

I know I can change any day
with my thoughts.
Every moment offers me an opportunity
to deny or embrace life.

MICHAEL BURGOS

It's A Comfort To Know
You Can Choose Your Attitude

Take responsibility for how you think and respond.

The world can be an irritating place – from the newspaper headlines bursting with bad news to the overfilled freeways to the clerk-with-attitude. Before we even realize it, we may have fallen into the chameleonlike habit of absorbing the anger, frustration and rudeness that crosses our paths and allowing these black emotions to color our internal monologue as well as our behavior.

That can make for a very unpleasant personal world.

The good news is we get to choose what we focus on. There will always be a beautiful sky overhead and a gutter with garbage at our feet. Don't worry – you're not denying the garbage exists by choosing to lift your eyes to the sky. Where you look is where you live.

We also get to choose our reactions. Although you cannot control the situations or people you encounter, you can choose how you respond to them. You always have "response-ability" (as coined by Dr. Wayne Dyer), which allows you to alter the emotional voltage of any situation.

Now *that* feels empowering, to say nothing of more pleasant.

IDEA Read, watch and listen to positive influences. Between the media and other people, you get enough negativity without even trying. So what do you get when you try? Putting a positive perspective into your head may take a deliberate decision and a trip to the bookstore or library for some input from the guru of your choice. It comes in all versions: books, tapes, CDs, videos, DVDs, calendars, cards – you name it. Now go get it.

IDEA Take on a "Student of the World" mentality. Every situation, no matter how stressful, can be an opportunity to learn something that will increase your wisdom and knowledge. Pretend for a day that whatever situation you encounter will enrich you, even though you won't know how until the day is over. Break your negative response habit and see what happens.

IDEA Make other people responsible for their own feelings. If someone is rude to you or speaks to you angrily, decide immediately that what they are exhibiting is their decision. Your response is your decision. Experiment: Try an empathetic reaction and see how their emotions might change.

IDEA Really count your blessings. Our lives consist of a constant series of events, so ferret out all the best stuff by focusing on your blessings as often as possible. Keep a dry erase blessing board, and either start your day by writing a blessing to think about throughout the day or end your day by recalling a blessing the day provided.

Start a Blessing Box by writing your blessings several times a week on slips of paper you put into a box or coffee can. Read them on Thanksgiving and you'll know what you're thankful for!

Choose Your Attitude And You Choose Your Life

Let The Good Things In Your Life Amaze You

Notice your blessings on purpose.

Patricia:
　　Years back, a young mother told me how she was keeping what she called a Blessing Box. She and her kids had decorated a jumbo coffee can and cut a large slit in the plastic top. They wrote down all the things that "went right" in their lives onto pieces of paper they popped into the can, then read the year's accumulation out loud every Thanksgiving.

　　What a concept! Turn Thanksgiving into an annual opportunity to review all the good events of the year that actually make you feel . . . thankful.

Hey, why would I ever want to stop noticing all the good things in my life?

　　I decided that was the best idea I'd heard in a long time and decorated my coffee can that night. My husband and young son and I turned the Blessing Box into a family tradition we looked forward to every year.

　　Flash-forward a decade. Although the husband and I have parted ways and our son is in his twenties and living his own grown-up life, I still keep my Blessing Box. I got addicted. Hey, why would I ever want to stop noticing all the good things in my life?

　　A good idea doesn't mean much if it doesn't work in reality, so I have to keep the Blessing Box where I can see it daily (out of sight, out of mind) and keep a pad of paper and a pen right there with it (if it's not convenient, it doesn't happen).

　　One year I found a playful pad of paper with alternating colors that has added a new symbolic element to the ritual. Taking the lid off my Blessing Box reveals all the grin-worthy memories from my life in a colorful bouquet of paper.

Blessings have no size limit: the car repair was only $75; you and your mate came out of a fight with a Nobel Peace Prize; your kid got a good grade; you had a superlative evening with friends over dinner. The important thing is that you are looking back over the last few days to find your blessings and, in the process, you and your family are learning what to value.

As I read all the blessings, I relive them in awe. Was that this year?

The Keeper Blessings, ones I choose to put back and read again next year, have turned into annual opportunities to remember special blessings that touch my heart. Some of them are brief but tender eulogies for a person or pet who has passed away. Sometimes they record a significant event, like purchasing a house, finishing school or (ahem!) getting a book published.

As I read all the blessings, I relive them in awe. Was that this year? Oh, I forgot about that one! I am overwhelmed with gratitude for the incredible year I have been given.

And what of the unhappy or "black cloud" events of the year? Ironically, my annual tradition reveals that with time passing, many of the things I thought were black cloud events provided the rain that turned barely seen seeds into this colorful bouquet of paper flowers.

Develop A Habit That Rewards You

105

How Do You Comfort Yourself?

Julianne, 14, Student

I listen to my favorite music in my room for a while, then go online to talk to friends to take my mind off of it and to have a laugh.

Janis, 54, Weight Watchers Receptionist

I do a few things – I play with my grandson, I pray, I take a walk, and sometimes I cry.

Christina, 20, Student

I think of all my good qualities, my family, my friends, my boyfriend, how I can resolve whatever sticky situation I may be in. I think of all the wonderful things I have in my life to be thankful for. I know God has blessed me in so many ways, and thinking of all my blessings always puts me in a good mood with a smile on my face. If all else fails, peanut butter comes in handy, too!

JJ, 58, Artist

I find it difficult to take time for myself, even when invited out by people I care about, because of all that I expect from myself every day.

I feel my comfort is having friends that I care about and some success in my chosen field. (In full honesty, when stressed, unhappy, conflicted or blocked, I clean: bathrooms, clothes, floors, windows – anything.)

Revive Empowerment

Fear paralyzes;

curiosity empowers.

Be more interested than afraid.

PATRICIA ALEXANDER

It's A Comfort To Revive
Your Feeling Of Empowerment

Do something that's a little risky.

If you haven't done anything emotionally brave in a while, you may have been slowly sapping away your ability to risk. When that happens, a person's world gets smaller and smaller. What starts out as a desire to be safe from conflict or stress can end up leaving you feeling as if you have no power.

When it gets to that point, it's imperative that you give yourself an opportunity to feel your own inner brave-heart. Remind yourself you're alive! Poke yourself in the comfort zone! Courage gives confidence – and confidence creates ease and opportunity for living your life to its best potential.

That said, what may seem like a small act of bravery to others can be a significant one for you, therefore, only you can determine what your act of bravery would look like.

IDEA Call an old friend you haven't spoken to in a while. You may feel embarrassed to have been out of touch for so long, but the odds are good that your friend feels the same way and will be overjoyed to talk to you again. If not – well, you can choose to feel good that you were brave enough to find out rather than spend the rest of your life wondering about it!

IDEA Do something you've never done before at least once a week. It's common to feel fear at the thought of trying something new or going somewhere you've never been. Don't let that stop you! Look at the local newspapers and deliberately pick

108

something to do or somewhere to go that's brand new to you. You don't have to go alone, but alone is fine, too – sometimes that's how you meet new people.

The act of expanding one's life is an act of courage that creates a magical momentum. You will feel the world outside you – and inside you – open wide.

IDEA Find counseling through your community or church, and work through something in your past that haunts you. Turning a stumbling block into a stepping-stone can be a two-person job. Even though you can't change the past, understanding it can help you make peace with it. Counseling is usually on a sliding scale to your income, so finances aren't an excuse. If it's pain you're afraid of, that's understandable, but don't let old hurts bully your future into being less than it can be.

Look for an objective counselor with whom you can develop a rapport. Think about the qualities you need in a professional that will make you receptive. It may be a gender preference, a religious affiliation or a personality type. Don't be surprised if it takes a couple of interviews or recommendations to find the counselor who's a good match for you.

It takes courage to face down an old hurt – but it's worth it. It's your life.

Face Down Fear

Revive An Old Friendship

Take a chance with someone you miss.

Michael:

Upon approaching my 45th birthday, I found myself facing an odd awareness. I hadn't spoken to some of my "good friends" for three or four years. I felt I had to make an important decision to think of them strictly as part of my past or do something to bring them into my present and my future.

In our mobile culture, when people we care about are in a distant place, it can take a conscious effort to maintain the connection of friendship and fondness. Not living in the same town easily leads to a drifting apart of interests, as well as a shrinking of shared experiences. This makes continuing personal intimacy something that is difficult and challenging.

It felt like a big risk to reach out to these people I had once loved.

I felt discomfort when I considered trying to contact these old friends, since contacting them was the obvious implication of a decision to keep their friendship. Whether it was a rational fear or not, I was afraid they might be angry and reject me. I was afraid the memory of the good times we'd had and the affection in our hearts had faded and perhaps been forgotten. I also wondered if they really did care about me anymore.

It felt like a big risk to reach out to these people I had once loved. And the longer I delayed in contacting them, the greater the sense of shame I felt. Shame is a powerful and uncomfortable feeling that easily creates procrastination. It would be a lot easier if I just shrugged and let it go.

Yet, I thought, friends are precious commodities, harder to find as we grow older. Established relationships, even if a little dusty, become precious.

110

I also raged against our cultural tendency to isolate ourselves. Shouldn't I take responsibility for turning that generality into specific action in my own life, no matter how uncomfortable it made me? Determined to follow through, to reach out and reconnect, I had a burst of bravery and chose an old friend from my Rolodex – only to realize, with irony, that the phone number I had was no longer current.

Thank God for the Internet! Two or three searches and up popped my friend's Web site. I cruised it and got the information I needed.

My bravery collapsed at this point. Even with my friend's current phone number and the continued prodding and encouragement from my mate (and my own conscience), it took two more weeks for me to get up the courage to make that call.

Shame is a powerful and uncomfortable feeling that easily creates procrastination.

When I did, I'd have recognized my friend's voice anywhere, just as he seemed to know mine. What a comfort it was to hear his enthusiasm and excitement, to sense his genuine receptivity to my call! He welcomed me back into his life wholeheartedly and we have spoken several times since, with plans to cross state lines and get together.

My worst fear of being rejected was simply that: fear. Unrealized and unexplored, the power of the fear remained strong.

That is, until it was dispelled through one courageous act.

When In Doubt, Reach Out

111

How Do You Comfort Yourself?

Helen, 46, University Instructor
Comfort is knowing that I am spiritually related to all creatures in this great universe in a way so intimate that I am shaken by the explosion of stars at the still hour of noon. It is the awesome sense of connectedness and belonging that I believe cannot be explained by anything other than God.

Trish, 52, Freelance Writer/Singer-Songwriter
Sometimes I write a letter to someone if that person has caused a disturbance in my life. I may not send it, but getting the feelings out generates clarity.

A change of scene is a big comfort for me, too -- helps me find new perspectives. Small adventures (large ones, too, if I can afford the time and money) are life-enhancing and mind-stretching.

Spending time with my son is a comfort for me. He's such a pal -- cheerful, playful and truly generous of spirit. Watching him interact with others, seeing people respond positively to him, makes me truly proud of who he has become and of my own accomplishment as a mother.

Rob, 56, Attorney
…seek out others for love and/or understanding.
…release emotion.

112

18

Embrace Maturity

Seekers are finders.

PATRICIA ALEXANDER

It's A Comfort To Embrace
Your Opportunity To Mature

Decide to purposefully pursue your inner peace.

Our culture seems to promote the belief that holding on to eternal youth is everyone's desire, that being a grown-up brings the collapse of a carefree lifestyle and mind-set. Yet the opposite is true, as we are not meant to be eternal children, choosing one extreme or the other.

Our choice is simple. Choose to evolve in our personhood or choose to stagnate.

While no one would consciously choose to stagnate, we all know someone older who is self-involved, petty, impatient and insensitive. To avoid this sad scenario for yourself, you must give yourself permission to evolve into the grown-up you were meant to be, without criticizing what that complex and sometimes painful process entails.

Rather than fearing or resisting your opportunity to mature, embrace it and begin an exciting journey toward self-acceptance – balance – and inner peace, something an eternal childhood could never deliver.

The gifts of maturity always await all who seek them. That is, indeed, a true comfort.

IDEA Read or listen to self-help books, seek classes, retreats or therapy. If you get stuck in an emotion that's taking you nowhere, such as fear, depression or resentment, you need some new perspectives to act as your tow truck. Do some research. Get the value of someone else's experience or research. Maturity increases when you

114

view uncomfortable negative emotions as opportunities to stretch and grow. It's always a choice and it's always yours.

IDEA Increase the affection and humor of your own inner voice. We all keep ourselves company in our heads, with a running commentary of our reactions and feelings to the world as we experience it. With a healthy maturity, your inner voice gains a perspective that is not as thin-skinned as one run on pure ego or as self-criticizing as one based on fear. Accepting our own human foibles, and flavoring that acceptance with affection and humor, enables us to increase our compassion to ourselves and others, and to enjoy our own company.

IDEA Give yourself credit for mature decisions. Instead of dwelling on your mistakes, make a list of all the important decisions you've made in your life that you can look back on and feel good about. Also look at all the mistakes that you transformed into valuable lessons. The person you are today was built on these moments. Be proud of yourself.

IDEA Harness your emotions with your intellect. Your feelings are real and should be acknowledged, but since your feelings may not represent the whole truth, allowing them to control your actions only creates chaos. Children are run by their feelings; adults temper their feelings with knowledge and logic. Stop, think, work it through, do research, seek opinions from trusted friends. That's maturity.

It's Actually A Comfort To Grow Up

115

Be On Alert For Your Own Rationalization Process

Decide how your actions define your character.

Michael:
Patricia and I once stayed in a four-star bed-and-breakfast at a winery. Even though they treated us like royalty, the little boy inside me wanted to get away with something, to get more than anybody else. So when we left, I included two wineglasses with the complimentary bottle of wine from our room.

I did this with a sense of playful glee because, after all, it was an upscale place and the wine was free, so why not the glasses, too? This wasn't such a great leap, I thought to myself. Many wineries give complimentary glasses.

Soon, I heard the voice of my conscience, as a strong feeling of discomfort.

As we checked out, I noticed the wineglasses on display, marked $12 a piece. In a moment of complete absurdity and rebellion, I also swiped a $16 souvenir coffee cup. Again, in my mind, an act of playfulness. I got away with it, didn't I? I paid good money for the stay, didn't I? These were my rationalizations.

Soon I heard the voice of my conscience as a strong feeling of discomfort. What I'd done was not acceptable behavior, and I had to admit I'd done it before. It was time to face this and grow up; I resolved not to do it again.

It was time to face this and grow up...

The next time I found myself at a pricey lodging, all I took home was the free bottle of wine. That felt better. This simple story is my lesson in maturity. I was doing something wrong. I examined my conscience. I resolved not to repeat it, and I followed through on the resolution.

P.S. I called the B&B later and told them to charge me for the wineglasses and the coffee cup. An embarrassing but cheap penance in the long run.

Have The Courage To Listen To Your Conscience

116

Turn Your Mistakes Into Life-Changing Decisions

Forgive yourself when you've learned a lesson.

Patricia:

It has been my life's lesson to learn the importance of being trustworthy with people's secrets. Two painful episodes burned this through to me.

The first was when I was only 19 and in college, majoring in drama, and working backstage on a show. I was thrilled to be befriended by an older girl in the cast, who confided something personal to me. With little thought, I repeated it; it made the rounds like brushfire, coming back to her in the form of a snide comment. She was so stunned, her eyes filled with tears, she ran from the room, and she never spoke to me again. When I realized that I had caused her pain with my careless betrayal, I felt as though a concrete block had landed on my chest. I swore to myself I would never tell another's secret again.

I felt as though a concrete block had landed on my chest.

But I did. I was 35 and, for no reason I understand, I told a male co-worker a criticizing remark about him that a female co-worker had told me in confidence. The man called her up and chastised her; she called me, quite angry.

I had no defense. Sick with regret, I felt disappointed in myself to my core. My heart ached like a bruise. I sent the woman a sincere note of apology and a huge basket of flowers. The next time I saw her, I immediately started to weep and I apologized again. She forgave me.

I swore to myself I would never tell another's secret again. But I did.

Eventually, I forgave myself. But only because my regret transformed into a solid resolve to grow up and be more trustworthy. I monitor my mouth carefully now and parent my chatty "inner child" to be more discreet. Twice was enough.

Transform Regret Into Resolve

117

How Do You Comfort Yourself?

Joanne, 46, Computer Consultant and Real Estate Professional
I started growing up and recognizing that I'm the one responsible for my own happiness.
I would feel guilty that I wasn't doing what I could to save my marriage. It was a therapist who helped me recognize my own self-worth and that I'm worthy of having someone around who would value me.

Carli, 54, Realtor
One way I relieve distress is by listening to positive thinking CDs from authors like Wayne Dyer, Lynn Grabhorn, Cherie Carter Scott, etc. It helps me get centered and have peace within my soul.

Larry, 55, Founder of Marketing/Coaching Firm
I try to decide if my discomfort is rational or irrational. If it's irrational, it's helpful to acknowledge that and remind myself not to focus on the irrational.
If it is rational, then I need to decide if it is a challenge I want to take on. If not, I try to let it go.
If I do take it on, I begin to write my thoughts and create an action plan.
It has been my experience that distress comes when I'm unclear. For me, clarity creates comfort.

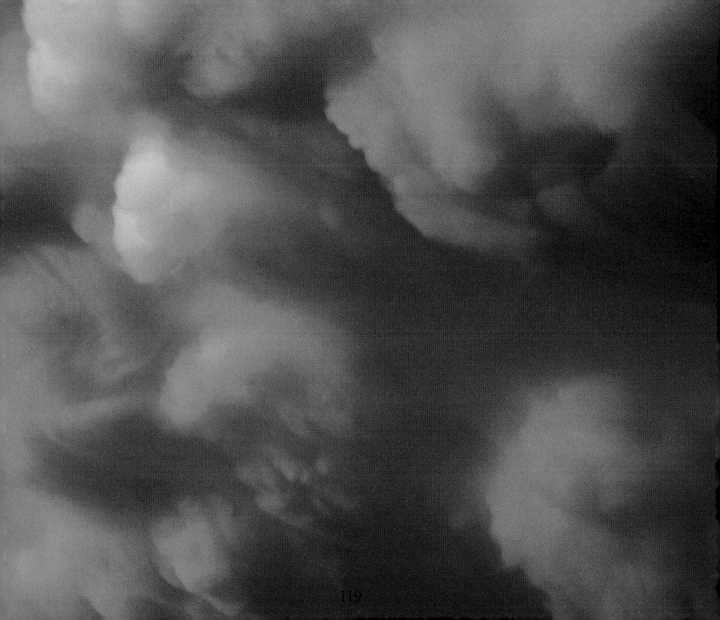

119

ABOUT THE CREATORS

PATRICIA ALEXANDER

Patricia has enjoyed a 30-year career as a professional writer, editor, journalist, marketing coach, speaker and humorist. Her writing experience includes entertainment segments of ABC's *Good Morning, America*, magazine and newspaper articles, business and marketing materials, advertising, public relations, and six years as a columnist for two newspapers, writing humorously about the human condition.

Her speaking and performing experience includes guest speaker to a variety of business organizations, seminar leader, certified Toastmaster and stand-up comic. She is also an ambassador to the media for a leading international weight loss organization, as well as a leader of weight loss meetings.

Overweight as a child, Patricia became a constant dieter. She hovered on the edge of poor self-esteem, rescued by supportive mentors, a natural optimism and her keen desire to be healthy in spirit, body and soul.

After her 23-year marriage ended, Patricia started an exciting journey towards the second half of her life. It began by finally discovering the way to healthy weight loss and shedding 40 pounds. During this process, she met Michael Burgos, whom she fondly calls Mr. B., and they merged their lives and their creative talents.

Writing a book about how people can comfort themselves has been an important part of that journey. Patricia's personal history, combined with her work as a weight loss teacher, has made her a champion cheerleader and dispenser of common sense and comfort.

MICHAEL BURGOS

Although originally interested in pursuing journalism, Michael's concurrent interest in psychology led him to receive two Master of Arts degrees, in Counseling Psychology and in Education. He is also a licensed Marriage and Family Therapist, who specialized as a Clinical Supervisor, training student therapists, and consulting on all their cases.

After fifteen years of helping people one-on-one, he felt an urgent need to share the fruits of his work and personal experiences in this book.

A strong, life-affirming spirit combined with a challenging medical history has led Michael to be especially attuned to other people's suffering and determinedly proactive about his own physical and emotional health.

When he was only two years old, he lost a kidney to cancer, and received radiation treatments that affected his immune system and bone structure. When he was 28, he had a lymphoma, receiving seven months of intensive chemotherapy. He has also struggled with constant back pain and sleep challenges, as well as Attention-Deficit/Hyperactivity Disorder (ADHD).

The result has been that he has sought comfort and health throughout his entire life. This, combined with his innate honesty and sense of humor, made him the perfect person to co-create this book.

123

DEAN ANDREWS

From the first moment of this book's conception, the authors wanted the art and design of their book to be as music is to a movie – subtle, interwoven, constant and affecting. Artist Dean Andrews has the spiritual maturity, creative experience and passion they were seeking.

Dean Andrews' paintings are in galleries and private collections across the country. In addition, she is an award winning art director, a graphic designer, creative director, illustrator, web site designer and creative consultant. Her varied background gives her the perfect perspective for blending fine art and graphic design.

Dean began her career as a graphic designer over 30 years ago and segued gradually to art director, then creative director. She worked for many years with J. Walter Thompson Advertising, where she put her mark of excellence on numerous national campaigns. She began focusing on her own work as a fine artist about 15 years ago, choosing to limit her art direction and design work to special projects that engaged her creative interest.

Dean's art is about light and space, and defines her as an innovator who uses a variety of mediums and techniques from Plexiglas to glass microspheres to reflective pigments. The paintings in this book are from her Strata series, small images of the sky, some literal, some more abstracted, all exuding tranquility and comfort. (To see more of her artwork, visit www.deanandrews.com.)

Not only does Dean bring her artist's creative focus to the book, but also her uninhibited fervor. She was committed to the process and excited to extend her paintings into the medium of print, merging her own vision with Patricia's and Michael's.

124

Artist's Statement

I have always been intrigued by the interaction of color and light, and how we perceive it; I am also fascinated with flying and with views of the sky seen from the sky. The Strata paintings incorporated in this book were inspired by both.

The artistic challenge has been to find ways of expressing in my painting what I am experiencing viscerally, as well as visually. Part of that challenge is to find materials that allow me to permanently capture my experience for others.

Like small views from an airplane window, these sky-inspired works are paintings on 9" x 14" Plexiglas that is one-inch thick. Each painting is slowly built up with 20-30 layers of transparent pigmented glazes that combine to create a remarkable spectrum of color. The translucent Plexiglas receives the light and incorporates it into the painting, illuminating the colored layers from within to create an ethereal, atmospheric effect.

As this book's graphic designer, I was charged with integrating the written concept with a visual one in a way that is aesthetically pleasing and engaging. I wanted *The Book of Comforts* to be graphically elegant and to take the reader on a personal adventure, whether bouncing from idea to anecdote, to quote to survey, or cruising pensively through the chapters from cover to cover. I designed each page carefully with this goal in mind, finding the section of each painting that would be best suited to the overall design.

It was clear from the start that the Strata series, these "little slices of sky," as they have been called, served our goal to combine words and art and create something that is not only a comfort to read, but also a comfort to behold.

125

STRATA SERIES

Strata XXVIII

Strata XXI

Strata XXX

Strata XIX

Strata XXXI

Strata XXIVV

Strata IX

Strata XVVII

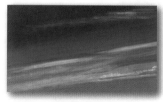

Strata XVIII

Strata XXVII

Strata XXXIII

Strata XXXII

Strata XXXV

Strata XV

Strata XXII

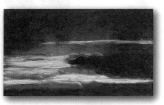
Strata XXXIV

Strata XXXVI

Strata XXXVI

How Do *You* Comfort Yourself?

Please tell us *your* answer to our survey question for possible use in future books!
E-mail your response to survey@bookofcomforts.com

For *The Book of Comforts* art and gifts, such as a Comfort Journal, Comfort Cards and more, visit our Web site at bookofcomforts.com.

May real comfort be yours!